American
Revolution
Almanac

American Revolution Almanac

Barbara Bigelow
and
Linda Schmittroth

Stacy A. McConnell, Editor

AN IMPRINT OF THE GALE GROUP

DETROIT · SAN FRANCISCO · LONDON
BOSTON · WOODBRIDGE, CT

Barbara Bigelow and Linda Schmittroth

Staff

Stacy A. McConnell *U•X•L Editor*
Julie L. Carnagie, *U•X•L Contributing Editor*
Carol DeKane Nagel, *U•X•L Managing Editor*
Thomas L. Romig, *U•X•L Publisher*

Margaret Chamberlain, *Permissions Specialist (Pictures)*
Maria Franklin, *Permissions Manager*

Rita Wimberley, *Senior Buyer*
Evi Seoud, *Assistant Production Manager*
Dorothy Maki, *Manufacturing Manager*
Tracey Rowens, *Art Director*
Pamela A. E. Galbreath, *Senior Art Director*

LM Design, *Typesetting*

Cover photographs (top to bottom): Abigail Adams reproduced by permission of Archive Photos; Paul Revere's ride reproduced by permission of Archive Photos; Thomas Jefferson holding the Declaration of Independence courtesy of The Library of Congress.

Library of Congress Cataloging-in-Publication Data
Schmittroth, Linda.

American Revolution: almanac / Linda Schmittroth; edited by Stacy McConnell.

p. cm.

Includes bibliographical references and index.

Summary: Provides in-depth background and interpretation of the American Revolution, with short biographies of people relevant to the topics discussed in each chapter.

ISBN 0-7876-3795-5

1. United States—History—Revolution, 1775-1783—Juvenile literature. 2. United States-History-Revolution, 1775-1783-Miscellanea-Juvenile literature. 3. Almanacs, American—Juvenile literature. [1. United States—History-Revolution, 1775-1783.] I. McConnell, Stacy A. II. Title.

E208.S28 2000

973.2-dc21   99-046939

Printed in the United States of America

10 9 8 7 6 5 4 3 2

Contents

Advisory Board

Special thanks are due for the invaluable comments and suggestions provided by U•X•L's American Revolution Reference Library advisors:

- Mary Alice Anderson, Media Specialist, Winona Middle School, Winona, Minnesota.

- Jonathan Betz-Zall, Children's Librarian, Sno-Isle Regional Library System, Edmonds, Washington.

- Frances Bryant Bradburn, Section Chief, Information Technology Evaluation Services, Public Schools of North Carolina, Raleigh, North Carolina.

- Sara K. Brooke, Director of Libraries, Ellis School, Pittsburgh, Pennsylvania.

- Peter Butts, Media Specialist, East Middle School, Holland, Michigan.

Reader's Guide

American Revolution: Almanac offers comprehensive commentary on the causes and progress of the American Revolution. The volume describes the American Revolution in terms that help students understand the events that led up to the war and why things happened as they did. It offers different viewpoints and interpretations of the events to help readers think about the larger themes and ideas surrounding the tremendous upheaval that was the Revolutionary War.

Arranged in twelve subject chapters, American Revolution: Almanac explores topics such as why the colonists came to the New World; colonial life before the Revolution; literature and arts of the Revolutionary period; the events that led up to the Revolution; the roles of Blacks and Native Americans in the war; the assembling of the Continental army; the Revolutionary War battles; and what brought the the war to a close.

Additional Features

American Revolution: Almanac includes numerous sidebars, some focusing on people associated with the Revolution, others taking a closer look at pivotal events of the time. More than sixty black-and-white illustrations and maps help to explain the text. Each chapter concludes with suggestions for further reading (fiction and nonfiction) about the events described in the chapter. The volume also contains a timeline, a glossary of terms used throughout the text, a bibliography of sources for further reading about the Revolution, research and activity ideas, and a cumulative subject index providing access to the subjects discussed throughout *American Revolution: Almanac*.

Acknowledgment

The authors wish to thank Mary Reilly McCall for her contribution of the research and activity ideas presented in this volume, and for the interest and enthusiasm she showed for the entire project.

Comments and Suggestions

We welcome your comments on this work as well as your suggestions for topics to be featured in future editions of *American Revolution: Almanac*. Please write: Editors, *American Revolution: Almanac*, U•X•L, 27500 Drake Rd., Farmington Hills, MI 48331-3535; call toll-free: 1-800-877-4253; fax: 248-699-8097; or send e-mail via www.galegroup.com.

Timeline of Events in Revolutionary America

1754   Start of the French and Indian War on the American frontier between the British and the French and their Native American allies.

1763   French and Indian War ends. Great Britain now controls New England colonies, the American frontier, and Canada.

1763   To maintain peace among the Native Americans on the frontier, King George III of England issues the Proclamation of 1763, forbidding colonists to settle in Native American territory west of the Appalachian Mountains.

1763   Still fearful that colonists will crowd onto their land, the Indians unite for Pontiac's Rebellion. Hundreds of pioneer families are killed before the rebellion is crushed by British soldiers.

1746
Benjamin Franklin
first begins
experiments with
electricity

1753
The Conestoga
wagon is
introduced

1756
The Seven
Years' War
begins

| 1745 | 1750 | 1755 | 1760 |

1764 British Parliament passes Sugar Act, forcing colonists to pay taxes on sugar, coffee, wine, dye, and other goods.

1764 James Otis publishes *Rights of the British Colonists Asserted,* arguing that "taxation without representation is tyranny."

1765 British Parliament passes the Stamp Act, which states that certain documents and other items must have stamps affixed to them or they are of no value.

1765 New York hosts the Stamp Act Congress; its members urge King George to repeal the hated Stamp Act.

1765 Colonial groups form to oppose the Stamp Act. Some adopt the name "Sons of Liberty." Outbreaks of violence occur, especially in Boston, Massachusetts.

1765 British Parliament passes the Quartering Act, which requires colonists to house and feed British soldiers.

1766 The Stamp Act is repealed, but the the British Parliament passes the Declaratory Act, stating that Parliament has a right to make any laws that would bind the colonists "in all cases whatsoever."

1767 King George's advisor Charles Townshend creates and Parliament passes the Townshend Acts, which place the heaviest taxes ever on the colonists.

1767 John Dickinson begins "Letters from a Farmer in Pennsylvania to Inhabitants of the British Colonies," pointing out that the Townshend Acts trample upon colonial rights.

1767 Massachusetts governor Thomas Hutchinson and other Massachusetts citizens begin to send letters to England describing the ugly mood in the colonies over British taxes.

1768 British soldiers are sent to keep the peace in Boston as the Sons of Liberty continue to incite angry crowds.

1763
The Seven Years'
War ends

1765
James Watt invents the
steam engine

1767
Joseph Priestly
pioneers carbonated
water

| 1762 | 1764 | 1766 | 1768 |

March 5, 1770 Five colonists are killed by British soldiers in the Boston Massacre. Not knowing of the massacre, Parliament does away with all of the Townshend taxes except the one on tea.

1772 In London, Benjamin Franklin receives a mysterious packet of letters written by Thomas Hutchinson. After reading the letters, Franklin believes that the British Parliament had taken harsh actions against the colonies at the urging of Hutchinson and others.

1772 An English judge decides the case of James Somersett, an American slave brought to England by his master. The judge finds that English law does not allow or approve of slavery. Slaves in America hear of this decision and grow restless.

1773 Parliament passes the Tea Act, another clear example of "taxation without representation."

December 16, 1773 In response to the Tea Act, Boston patriots dump 342 chests of tea into Boston Harbor in what becomes known as the Boston Tea Party.

1774 Thomas Jefferson publishes *Summary View of the Rights of British America*.

1774 Riots break out in Boston after the British Parliament passes the Intolerable Acts to punish Bostonians for the Boston Tea Party.

September 1774 The First Continental Congress meets in Philadelphia and approves the Declaration and Resolves, which states that colonists will stop buying British goods until their complaints are settled.

April 1775 The first shots of the Revolutionary War are fired at Lexington and Concord, Massachusetts. American soldiers force British troops back to Boston.

May 1775 The Second Continental Congress meets in Philadelphia to prepare for war. Ethan Allen and Bene-

---

1771
The first *Encyclopaedia Britannica* is published

1773
Phillis Wheatley's first book of poems is published

1775
Alexander Cummings receives first patent for a flush toilet

| 1770 | 1772 | 1774 | 1776 |

dict Arnold take Fort Ticonderoga, New York, from the British, although congress has not ordered it and war has not been declared.

June 1775 The Battle of Bunker Hill is fought on Breed's Hill overlooking Boston, marking the first real battle of the Revolutionary War. Congress appoints George Washington commander in chief of a yet-to-be formed Continental army.

July 1775 Congress adopts the Declaration of the Causes and Necessity of Taking Up Arms but also makes one last attempt to avoid a break with Great Britain by sending King George the Olive Branch Petition.

August 1775 King George issues a Proclamation of Rebellion and congress sends men to the frontier to request that the Native Americans remain neutral in any conflict with Great Britain.

September 1775 George Washington complains to congress that he has no money to pay his men and fears they will desert. Congress sends a committee to discuss the situation and steps are taken to provide money and supplies, while plans are made to build up an army of 20,000 men by calling on all the colonies.

October 1775 Fearing a slave uprising if he allows any blacks to serve, Washington issues an order barring free black men from joining the Continental army.

October 1775 The town of Falmouth (now Portland), Maine, a landing spot for American smugglers, is destroyed by British warships.

1776 Cherokee Indians stage the first Indian uprising of the Revolution against settlers in Georgia and the Carolinas.

January 1, 1776 Norfolk, Virginia, is destroyed by British warships.

1774	1775	1777
Ann Lee founds Shakerism	The first house rats recorded in America appear	Joseph Bramah patents the water closet

1774   **1775**   **1776**   **1777**

January 10, 1776 Thomas Paine publishes *Common Sense*. In it he calls King George III "the Royal brute of Great Britain."

March 2, 1776 Washington launches an attack on British-occupied Boston. Fifteen days later British general William Howe abandons Boston and heads to Canada.

April 1776 Washington and his troops fortify New York City, Howe's next target.

June 7, 1776 Congressman Richard Henry Lee reads a resolution in congress suggesting that relations between America and Great Britain be dissolved. It is passed the next month.

July 4, 1776 The Declaration of Independence is adopted, and it is read publicly to Washington's soldiers in New York five days later.

August 27, 1776 Howe's troops drive Americans from Long Island, New York, to Brooklyn Heights, New York.

September 6-7, 1776 Washington orders the launching of David Bushnell's submarine in an attack on the British navy off Staten Island, New York.

September 12, 1776 The Americans abandon New York City and retreat through New Jersey, fighting all the way to Pennsylvania.

September 22, 1776 American spy Nathan Hale is executed by the British without a trial.

December 12, 1776 Congress flees from Philadelphia to Baltimore to escape the approaching British army.

December 26, 1776 Washington stages a surprise attack on England's hired Hessian (German) soldiers at Trenton, New Jersey; the attack is a complete success.

January 3, 1777 Washington and his troops defeat British soldiers at Princeton. As a result, all British forts in central

1778	1779	1780	
The "sandwich" is invented	Jan Ingehousz studies photosynthesis	London's first Sunday newspapers appear	
1778	1779	1780	1781

and western New Jersey are abandoned, and Washington's New Jersey campaign is hailed as brilliant.

January 18, 1777 Congress makes public for the first time the names of the signers of the Declaration of Independence.

March 14, 1777 Washington writes to Congress that he has fewer than 3,000 men left and many are sick from smallpox and starvation. By the end of the year, Washington's ranks swell to their greatest number in the war.

July 5, 1777 British general John Burgoyne and his troops capture Fort Ticonderoga, New York, during what became known as Burgoyne's Offensive.

September 26, 1777 British general William Howe and his troops occupy Philadelphia.

September 19, 1777 Burgoyne fights American generals Horatio Gates and Benedict Arnold at Freeman's Farm in the first of two battles at Saratoga.

October 17, 1777 Burgoyne surrenders at Saratoga, New York

December 1777 The British retire for the winter in comfort in Philadelphia, while Washington and his army begin an agonizing winter at Valley Forge, Pennsylvania.

December 17, 1777 King Louis of France agrees to recognize American independence, which paves the way for France to openly help the American cause.

June 1778 The first French navy fleet arrives off the coast of Virginia. Fearful that the French navy will cut him off from British headquarters in New York, General Henry Clinton (who replaced Howe) abandons Philadelphia and heads for New York.

December 1778 Savannah, Georgia, falls to the British during the Southern campaign.

1774	1777	1779
Joseph Preistly discovers oxygen	Vermont prohibits slavery	War of Bavarian Sucession ends

| 1773 | 1775 | 1777 | 1779 |

June 30, 1779 Clinton promises certain freedoms to blacks who side with the British, and, as a result, tens of thousands of slaves flee behind British lines.

September-October 1779 Patriots try to retake Savannah with the help of the French navy. Their efforts fail and patriot spirits sink.

December 1779 Without proper food and supplies, Washington's army begins another terrible winter, this time at Morristown, New Jersey.

July 10, 1780 5,500 French troops arrive in Newport, Rhode Island, and practice military maneuvers with American soldiers.

December 1780 British general Charles Cornwallis heads for Virginia, believing its capture will win the war.

January 5, 1781 British troops under the command of former American general Benedict Arnold easily take Richmond, Virginia.

August 1781 Cornwallis prepares to defend Yorktown, Virginia, against an expected attack by Washington's army and French troops.

September 5, 1781 The French navy engages the British navy in battle. The French are victorious, and the British navy is not able to help Cornwallis defend Yorktown.

September 26, 1781 American and French troops surround Yorktown.

October 18, 1781 Cornwallis surrenders at Yorktown, ending the war.

September 3, 1783 The Treaty of Paris is signed, in which the British grant the colonies independence from British rule.

November 3, 1783 Washington says goodbye to his men and the Continental army is disbanded.

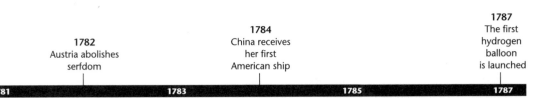

1782
Austria abolishes
serfdom

1784
China receives
her first
American ship

1787
The first
hydrogen
balloon
is launched

| 1781 | 1783 | 1785 | 1787 |

Words to Know

A

Abolitionism: The belief that measures should be taken to end slavery.

Absolutism: A system in which one person—usually a king or queen—rules without any kind of restrictions on his or her actions.

Agent: A person who conducts business on another's behalf.

Allegiance: Loyalty to king, country, or a cause.

Articles of Confederation: An agreement among the thirteen original states, approved in 1781, that provided a loose form of government before the present Constitution went into effect in 1789.

Artillery: The science of using guns; a group of gunners in an army; or the weapons themselves, especially cannons that throw bombs across a battlefield.

Assemblies: One of the names used by the colonies for their lawmaking bodies.

B

Boston Massacre: A encounter between British troops and townspeople in Boston in 1770, before the Revolutionary War. The British fired into a crowd and five Americans were killed.

Boston Tea Party: An incident on December 16, 1773, in which Boston patriots dumped 342 chests of English tea into Boston Harbor to protest British taxes.

Boycott: A refusal to buy, sell, or use certain products from a particular company or country, usually for a political reason.

Brigadier general: A military position just below major general.

Burgesses: An old term for members of the British Parliament; the lawmaking body of colonial Virginia called itself the House of Burgesses.

C

Cavalry: Soldiers on horseback.

Coercive Acts: The British name for the Intolerable Acts.

Colonel: A military rank below brigadier general.

Colonial agents: Men appointed by lawmaking bodies in the colonies to live in London, circulate among important people, and report back on what was happening in Parliament.

Colonialism: The extension of the power of a nation beyond its own borders.

Colonies: Territories that are settled by emigrants from a distant land that remain subject to or closely connected with the parent country.

Committees of Correspondence: Colonial groups that shared information, coordinated the activities of colonial agitators, and organized public opinion against the British government.

Committees of Safety: One of many colonial committees that had the authority to call up militias (groups of volunteer soldiers) when they were needed.

Confederation: A group of states united for a common purpose.

Conservatives: People who wish to preserve society's existing institutions.

Continental army: The army of American colonists formed during the American Revolution.

Continental Congress: An assembly of delegates from the American colonies (later states) that governed before and during the Revolutionary War and under the Articles of Confederation.

D

Declaration of Independence: The document establishing the United States as a nation, adopted by the Continental Congress on July 4, 1776.

Declatory Act: A law stating that the British government had the power to make laws that would bind the colonists "in all cases whatsoever."

Delegates: Representatives.

Democracy: A system of government in which power belongs to the people, who rule either directly or through freely elected representatives.

Duties: Taxes on imported or exported goods.

F

Federalist: One who supports a strong central government instead of a loose organization of states.

Founding Fathers: A general name for male American patriots during the Revolutionary War, especially the signers of the Declaration of Independence and the drafters of the Constitution.

Freedom of the press: The right to circulate opinions in print without government interference.

French and Indian War: A series of military battles between Great Britain and France (and France's Native American allies) that took place on the American frontier and in Canada between 1754 and 1763.

French Revolution: An event lasting from 1789 to 1799 that ended the thousand-year rule of kings in France and established France as a republic.

G

Great Britain: The island off the western coast of Europe made up of England, Scotland, and Wales. Also called "Britain" or "England."

Grievances: Complaints.

H

Hessians: German soldiers hired by King George III to fight for the British during the American Revolution. Many came from Hesse-Cassel, and, as a result, all German soldiers were called Hessians.

I

Infantry: Men with handguns.

Intolerable Acts: Four laws passed by the British government in 1774 to punish Boston for the Boston Tea Party.

L

Loyalists: Colonists who remained loyal to England during the Revolution; also known as Tories.

M

Martial law: Temporary rule by military authorities imposed upon regular citizens in time of war or when civil authority has stopped working.

Mercenaries: Soldiers for hire.

Militia: A military force consisting of citizens rather than professional soldiers.

Minutemen: Armed American citizens (nonmilitary) who promised to be ready to fight alongside regular soldiers at a moment's notice.

Monarchy: Rule by a king or queen.

Musket: A type of shoulder gun that shoots bullets resembling balls.

N

Neutral: Not committed to either side of an issue.

New England: The region in the northeastern United States that includes present-day Connecticut, Maine, Massachusetts, New Hampshire, Rhode Island, and Vermont. The name was probably given by English explorer John Smith, one of the original settlers of Jamestown, Virginia (1607), because the region resembled the coast of England.

New World: A European term for North and South America.

P

Parliament: The British lawmaking body.

Patriot: A person who loves, supports, and defends his country.

Petition: A formal document making a request.

Privateer: A sailor on a privately owned ship who is authorized by the government to attack and capture enemy vessels.

Propaganda: Biased or distorted information spread by persons who wish to present only their point of view and thus further their own cause.

Q

Quaker: A member of the Religious Society of Friends, which oppose all violence and warfare.

R

Radical: A person who favors revolutionary changes in a nation's political structure.

Rebel: A person who resists or defies ruling authority.

Redcoats: British soldiers, who wore red uniforms.

Republic: A form of government in which people hold the power and exercise it through elected representatives.

Resolution: A formal statement of a decision or expression of opinion put before or adopted by a lawmaking assembly.

Revenue: Money collected to pay for the expenses of government.

Revolution: A sudden political overthrow; a forcible substitution of rulers.

Revolutionary War: The conflict lasting from 1775 to 1783 in which American colonists gained independence from British rule.

S

Sedition: Acts or language leading to rebellion.

Separation of church and state: The principle that government must maintain an attitude of neutrality toward religion.

Six Nations Iroquois Confederacy: An Association of six Native American tribes: the Mohawk, Oneida, Onondaga, Cayuga, Seneca, and Tuscarora.

Stamp Act: A law passed by the British government in 1765 that required the payment of a tax to Great Britain on papers and documents produced in the colonies.

T

Thirteen colonies: The colonies that made up the original United States upon the signing of the Declaration of Independence in 1776: Connecticut, Delaware, Georgia, Maryland, Massachusetts, New Hampshire, New Jersey, New York, North Carolina, Pennsylvania, Rhode Island, South Carolina, and Virginia.

Tories: Colonists who remained loyal to England during the Revolution; also called Loyalists.

Townshend Acts: Laws passed by the British government in 1767. They included a Quartering Act, which ordered the colonies to house British troops, and a Revenue Act, which called for taxes on lead, glass, paint, tea, and other items.

Treason: Betrayal of king and country.

Tyranny: Absolute power, especially power exercised cruelly or unjustly.

Y

Yankee: Once a nickname for people from the New England colonies, the word is now applied to anyone from the United States.

Research and Activity Ideas

The following list of research and activity ideas is intended to offer suggestions for complementing social studies and history curricula, to trigger additional ideas for enhancing learning, and to suggest cross-disciplinary projects for library and classroom use.

Activity 1: A "live" historical event

Assigment: For a school assembly program dramatize an important event of the Revolutionary era. Base your dramatization on historical facts, although you are free to use your own dialogue and interpretation when necessary. Your goal is both to inform and entertain your audience. You must also involve each member of the class in the project.

Preparation: The first task is to choose an historical event. Possibilities include the Boston Massacre, the Boston Tea Party, or George Washington crossing the Delaware. To make a decision you might put the question to a class vote. Once you have chosen the event, you need to gather information for a script and other aspects of the dramatization. One approach is to form teams that will do research on a particular aspect of the event.

Using *American Revolution: Almanac* as a starting point, the teams must find information at the library and on Internet Web sites. Look for historical accounts of the event that can provide a narrative frame for your dramatization. Also look for documents from the period that can be used as the basis of speaking parts.

Presentation: When all teams have gathered their information, assign roles and responsibilities, such as script writers, a director, a narrator, major and minor speakers, "extras" for crowd scenes—perhaps even a publicity team, costume and prop crews, and lighting and sound crews, depending on the complexity of your production. Be sure everyone in the class is involved and concentrate on making the dramatization both informative and entertaining.

Activity 2: Revolutionary newspaper

Assignment: Prepare a special Revolutionary War issue of your local newspaper. This special issue could contain articles describing some of the pivotal events and people of the Revolutionary era; what life is like for the soldiers on the battlefields; and how women, Native Americans, and African Americans contribute to the war effort. Be sure that your articles contain not only the facts, but are also interesting to read.

Preparation: Hold a class story meeting to decide what article topics you want to present in your newspaper, as well as other items such as advertisements and classified ads. Assign people to the various jobs such as researchers, reporters, and editors.

Using *American Revolution: Almanac* as a starting point, look for additional information at the library and on Internet Web sites. Documents from the era can be used as the basis for your articles. For instance, diary entries may provide a good account of what it was like for people living during the war, while historians' accounts may provide good descriptions of battles and other events important to the Revolution.

Presentation: When all the research for the articles has been gathered, reporters assigned to each article can begin writing, while editors proofread the articles. The class can then decide on the layout of the newspaper. You may even include illustrations found by the researchers if you want your newspaper to be more authentic.

Activity 3: What if...

Assignment: What if the colonies had lost the American Revolution and remained under British rule? How would things be different in the United States today? It is your job to find out. Prepare a brochure and presentation that can be given to people from other countries who are thinking of moving to the United States. Your brochure and presentation should explain what these people's lives would be like if they chose to move to a United States that was still under British rule.

Prepartation: Using *American Revolution: Almanac* as a starting point, gather information about what things you think would be different if the United States was ruled by Britain. Consult your library and Internet Web sites for additional material. As you conduct your research, focus on government, religion, education, community and family life, food, and other relevant topics.

Presentation: After you have gathered your information, prepare your brochure and presentation. Be sure to make it both informative and entertaining so that you engage your audience. Also, keep in mind that you want to be as realistic as possible about what would be different about living in the United States if it was still a British colony. Use slides or overheads to enhance your presentation.

The People of the New World

Although English exploration of the North American continent began at the turn of the sixteenth century, the English did not establish permanent settlements in the vast New World territory until much later. (The New World is a European term for North and South America.)

Those who chiseled out new lives for themselves in the wilderness of North America did so for various reasons—to gain religious freedom, to obtain jobs, to take advantage of new farming opportunities, to enjoy a better standard of living than the overpopulated country of England could offer, even to try their hand at "get rich quick" schemes in the bountiful New World.

As word of the New World's ample resources got back to Great Britain, colonizing companies were established with money from British investors. (Colonialism is the extension of the power of a nation beyond its own borders.) By 1588 England had become the dominant power in Europe, and the island nation's colonial interests began to expand. In 1606 King James I of England (1566–1625; reigned 1603–1625)

Ample natural resources prompted many colonists to set up farms. Here a colonial family harvests their wheat crop.
(Reproduced by permission of Corbis Corporation [Bellevue].)

approved a charter for an agricultural and trade company to be set up in North America along the Atlantic coastline. The first permanent English colony was founded at Virginia the next year; its center, the Jamestown settlement, was located on a small peninsula surrounded by a marsh. The colony's economy grew around tobacco farming and export.

About a dozen years later, a group of Christian reformers known as Pilgrims were beginning a new life north of Virginia, in what would later be known as the New England colonies. Disillusioned with the Church of England (which was formed by King Henry VIII when he could not obtain an annulment of his marriage to Catherine of Aragon from the Roman Catholic Church; an annulment is an official declaration that a marriage is invalid), the Pilgrims had called for religious reform. They advocated simplicity and purity in religion and sought to free the church from corruption and political influence. But the reformists soon became the targets of religious persecution in their own country. Their strong desire to worship in an atmosphere of religious tolerance prompted them to leave England and head for the New World.

The Pilgrims landed in Cape Cod harbor in the fall of 1620. Guided by the democratic (government by the people) principles of their Mayflower Compact (named for the ship on which they sailed from England), they established their own government and formed a new religious society.

The earliest signs of colonial unrest—still considered mild unrest at this point—began to show in 1651, following the passage of the Navigation Acts by the British government. The Navigation Acts dictated that the colonies existed for the benefit of the Mother Country (England) and that the colonies' trade should be restricted to the Mother Country. Only British-owned ships with a British crew could import goods from Asia, Africa, and America into Great Britain, Ireland, or other British colonies. These acts hampered the colonies' overseas trade, prompted a rash of smuggling, and foreshadowed England's attempts to increase its control over the colonies.

Tensions mount

Meanwhile, the issue of Native American tribal rights to New World land became more and more volatile. Native American resistance to English settlement reached a fever pitch by the mid-1670s. Relations between the colonists and the Native Americans had been uneasy for years because of colonial expansionism: land-grabbing colonists pushed the Native tribes out of their homeland all along the eastern seaboard, leading to a bloody two-year-long conflict known as King Philip's War (1675–76).

Over the following decades, tensions arose between the French and English colonists in the New World. The French and Indian War (1754–63) broke out when French forces from Canada tried to take over the Ohio Valley. The French and their Indian allies fought against the English—a combined force of American colonists and British soldiers—for control of the area. (In 1756 the fighting spread to the European continent, where the conflict came to be known as the Seven Years' War.) Although the American/English troops suffered serious setbacks in the mid- to late 1750s, by war's end the French had lost Canada and their holdings in the Ohio Valley.

King George of England on top of the world

On February 10, 1763, twenty-four-year-old King George III (1738–1820; reigned 1760–1820), barely three years on the British throne, was feeling on top of the world. His representatives were in Paris, France, signing the peace treaty that ended the brutal Seven Years' War. At this point, England's flag flew in North America and in parts of the Caribbean, Africa, and India. It was a glorious time for the British Empire. Great Britain was the most powerful nation in the world. The population of her vast North American possessions had grown to 1.5 million people, and many of them remained loyal to King George. With America's western frontier free of threats from the French, American colonists saw a great continent open to them for exploration and settlement. They hoped to expand westward—on their own terms.

Immigration to the New World just before the Revolution

The population of the thirteen American colonies grew enormously from 1700 to 1776. Black Africans made up more than one-half of the immigrants to the colonies, though they did not come willingly. They were captured from their native Africa, shackled, loaded by the thousands onto filthy ships, and sent across the ocean to perform slave labor for wealthy white landowners.

A majority of the other immigrants arrived from Great Britain (England, Scotland, and Wales) and Ireland (one of the British Isles; see box titled "Immigration by Country, 1700–1775"). Most people journeyed to the New World to escape the endless wars and conflicts in their homelands (in some countries, men were actually seized off the streets and forced to serve in armies) or to find honest work and create better lives for themselves and their children. Some were looking for a place where they could worship God in their own way. All

Immigration by Country, 1700–1775[1]

Except for African slaves, who were kidnaped and sent to the Americas against their will, newcomers to the New World in the seventy-five years before the American Revolution came mainly from Germany, England, Scotland, and Ireland.

Decade	Africans	Germans	N. Irish[2]	S. Irish	Scots	English	Welsh	Other	Total
1700–1709	9,000	100	600	800	200	400	300	100	11,500
1710–1719	10,800	3,700	1,200	1,700	500	1,300	900	200	20,300
1720–1729	9,900	2,300	2,100	3,000	800	2,200	1,500	200	22,000
1730–1739	40,500	13,000	4,400	7,400	2,000	4,900	3,200	800	76,200
1740–1749	58,500	16,600	9,200	9,100	3,100	7,500	4,900	1,100	110,000
1750–1759	49,600	29,100	14,200	8,100	3,700	8,800	5,800	1,200	120,500
1760–1769	82,300	14,500	21,200	8,500	10,000	1,900	7,800	1,600	157,800
1770–1775	17,800	5,200	13,200	3,900	15,000	7,100	4,600	700	67,500
TOTAL	278,400	84,500	66,100	42,500	35,300	44,100	29,000	5,900	585,800

[1]All figures are approximate.

[2]The Northern Irish, sometimes called Scots-Irish, were Scots who were sent in the 1600s by the British to settle in Northern Ireland and help dominate the Catholic Irish who lived there.

Source: Aaron S. Fogleman, Hopeful Journeys: German Immigration, Settlement, and Political Culture in Colonial America, 1717–1775. Philadelphia: University of Pennsylvania, 1996. In American Eras: The Revolutionary Era, by Robert J. Allison. Detroit: Gale, 1998, p. 235.

had an uncommon sense of drive and adventure—qualities lacking in many of their neighbors who stayed behind.

Settlement patterns in the New World

About 40 percent of the New World settlers from Germany established homes in Pennsylvania, while others scattered throughout the Middle and Southern colonies. The Germans were known as hardworking and thrifty farmers. The Scots and Scots-Irish (Scots who moved to Ireland in the 1600s) settled in the backcountry (away from cities) of North and South Carolina and along the Hudson River Valley of New York. The Irish settled in the backcountry extending from South Carolina northward to Maine.

The backcountry was a remote and unsettled wilderness. People who set up lodgings there were tough and independent-minded and wanted nothing to do with the burgeoning colonial government. They lived ruggedly and survived by hunting, fishing, and picking wild fruits and greens.

The land and the homes of colonial Americans

The whole of European society was rooted in a tradition of unequal distribution of land, and one of the great attractions of the American colonies was the opportunity they offered for land and home ownership. Such opportunities varied from colony to colony, however, with the best being available in New England. As a London newswriter observed in 1767: "Every one in the New England colonies is a freeholder, and enjoys more liberty than any other people in Europe and America." In this passage, the word "every one" does not include women and blacks—only white males. (Freeholders generally hold their land for life, but in New England, settlers could subdivide their land to their children or sell it.)

The situation in the Middle and Southern colonies was less equitable. A small number of individuals in New York, New Jersey, Maryland, and Virginia were awarded huge parcels of land by the British government, and great castles and plantation homes were constructed there. Farmers and frontier settlers made do with smaller plots of land and far more modest homes.

People in the New England colonies designed their homes to be practical rather than beautiful. The design took into account the local weather conditions and building materials available. New England houses were built out of the plentiful wood, with small, low-ceilinged rooms that were easy to keep warm in winter. The look of some of the houses had a decidedly European flavor.

In New York along the Hudson River, a region originally settled by the Dutch, houses were often constructed in the narrow style similar to that of Dutch towns. New York dwellings were usually built out of wood and stone rather than the traditional Dutch brick and tile. Brick, however, was the favorite building material in the Middle and Southern colonies. After suffering a great fire in 1740, Charleston, South Carolina, was rebuilt almost entirely in brick and Spanish concrete, made from oyster shells, sand, and water.

As Northern merchants, Southern planters, and government officials grew wealthy in the mid-eighteenth century, they sought to display their wealth through their houses and the other luxury items they owned. Americans with a knowledge of European architecture—and plenty of money—built many impressive and elegant houses. The best known was future American president Thomas Jefferson's (1743–1826) Virginia home, Monticello. A scholar, author, statesman, and naturalist, the multitalented Jefferson counted among his gifts a knowledge of architecture. He began the building of Monticello in 1771 and perfected the home over the next forty years.

Lifestyles of wealthy colonials before the Revolution

Class structure was very much alive in the colonial period. Compared to London society, living conditions in the colonies were crude, but this did not stop wealthy colonists from aspiring to a high standard of living. The wealthy spent their time and money imitating European habits and tastes, especially those popular in the court of French King Louis XV.

Acquiring an air of good manners and breeding took years. Among the less wealthy, etiquette (pronounced ETT-uh-kitt) books, which explained codes of behavior and courtesy, were popular reading. Those who wished to fit in among the wealthy went to tutors to learn proper speech, to acquire information on art and music, and to practice fencing (fighting with swords) and dancing.

After the French and Indian War ended in 1763, more luxury goods were produced and consumed in America than ever before. These included the latest in clothing styles, ornate carriages with uniformed drivers, and fine houses furnished in mahogany wood and fine china. The colonists were not shy about displaying their wealth for all to see.

Although they were separated by an ocean, wealthy colonists imitated the habits and fashion of French men and women in the court of Louis XV.

(Reproduced by permission of Archive Photos, Inc.)

While many wealthy women spent most of their time confined to the house, wealthy men spent their days conducting business and moving about town. Many men exhibited their wealth through their manner of dress. They wore close-fitting coats and knee breeches (trousers that extended to or just below the knee) woven from brightly colored silks and velvets. Collars and cuffs were trimmed with lace, and stockings were made of white silk.

The most important sign of a true gentleman was his powdered wig, usually made from women's hair, smeared with animal fat, curled with a hot iron, rolled, and dusted with plaster of paris (a type of cement powder) or flour. Middle-class lawyers, doctors, and shopkeepers who could not afford the expense of such a wig had theirs made of horse or goat hair. The wigs were hot, heavy, and uncomfortable, and they often released small showers of white powder when the wearers moved. Men had to take lessons to learn how to keep the wigs on and walk at the same time.

Women wore French corsets—a type of close-fitting undergarment that molds and shapes the upper body—and low-cut gowns. Before the style changed in the 1770s, women kept their hair covered with hoods or caps. Later, they sported large, powdered hairdos given height and fullness with "rats" or hairpieces that were glued on. Arranging such a hairdo took so much time that it was done only once a month or so. In between, women slept with their necks resting on wooden blocks to avoid ruining the look.

Dancing was the most important element in the social life of the wealthy. Balls were held quite frequently, and a person's level of refinement and sophistication was closely tied to his or her ability to dance with style and grace. In the New World, unlike the Old, a humble man who could dance well could sometimes rise above his station by catching the eye and heart of a wealthy young maiden and marrying her.

Occupations of pre-Revolutionary-era slaves

     In sharp contrast to the extravagant lives of wealthy whites in early colonial America, the situation for black African slaves was appalling. In the seventy-five years prior to the American Revolution, 278,400 Africans were brought by force to the American colonies to serve as slaves. They made up more than one-half of the immigrants to the New World in that period. The rapidly growing economy was in need of a labor force, and black Africans were chosen to fill a huge part of that need. At the start of the war, black slaves made up the second-largest occupational group in America—second only to white farmers.

     Slave women performed the worst of the tasks. They toiled in the fields on Maryland and Virginia tobacco plantations and on small Pennsylvania farms. They performed the difficult jobs of cultivating rice and indigo (a plant that yields

Many wealthy colonial men believed that "true gentlemen" wore powdered wigs. Because of the heaviness of these awkward hairpieces, new wearers often took lessons to learn how to dance and walk while wearing them.
(Reproduced by permission of The Granger Collection, New York.)

a substance for making blue dye) in the Carolinas and Georgia. They spun and wove wool and flax, washed, ironed, cooked, and milked cows in Northern towns. In the rural North, the women performed all the household tasks and also preserved fruit, made maple sugar, and worked in the fields when needed.

In the South, the children of black slave women helped build up a servant class, so slave women of childbearing age were especially prized by slaveholders. In addition to their work for their owners, the women tried to maintain their own family lives and cultural traditions, all in the face of overwhelming odds. Family members could be sold off on a master's whim, and tensions often arose in black families when women were cruelly used or otherwise violated by their white owners.

In the North, black slave women who could perform a variety of different housekeeping tasks, such as cooking and sewing, were considered the most valuable. The demand for the labor of women and their children who could not perform such household tasks was low in the North, so marriage and childbearing among blacks were discouraged there.

Slave men performed skilled agricultural work. They sowed seeds and plowed fields. They also fished, processed and manufactured flour and grain in mills, and worked on sailing ships. Those trained as blacksmiths made, repaired, and fitted horseshoes; those trained as coopers constructed wooden tubs, casks, and barrels. Male slaves also worked as carpenters, cooks, and gardeners.

The life of a slave was a hard one, and after the American Revolution broke out in 1775, many slaves took advantage of wartime confusion to escape from bondage. Even some of American leader George Washington's slaves fled, including Deborah Squash and her husband, Harry, who sailed away from the so-called land of liberty on a British ship rather than continue to live in slavery.

How the working class got by

Class divisions became more pronounced in the colonies in the second half of the eighteenth century. The French and Indian War (1754–63) created a class of wealthy

Slaves' Petition for Freedom

In 1773 a new nation was on the brink of being born. Its people demanded freedom and a voice in their government—rights that were denied to African Americans, both slave and free. A small but active movement to end slavery was beginning to take shape, though, especially in the North. Members of the free black community did not remain silent as talk of liberty swirled around them. The petition below was presented to the Boston legislature on April 20, 1773.

Sir, The efforts made by the legislature of this province in their last sessions to free themselves from slavery, gave us, who are in that deplorable state, a high degree of satisfaction. We expect great things from men who have made such a noble stand against the designs of their fellow-men to enslave them. We cannot but wish and hope Sir, that you will have the same grand object, we mean civil and religious liberty, in view in your next session. The divine spirit of freedom, seems to fire every humane breast on this continent....

We are very sensible that it would be highly detrimental [it would cause harm]

to our present masters, if we were allowed to demand all that of right belongs to us for past services; this we disclaim [give up our rights to]. Even the Spaniards, who have not those sublime ideas of freedom that English men have, are conscious that they have no right to all the services of their fellow-men, we mean the Africans, who they have purchased with their money; therefore they allow them one day in a week to work for themselves, to enable them to earn money to purchase the [remainder] of their time...

In behalf of our fellow slaves in this province, and by order of their Committee.

> Peter Bestes
> Sambo Freeman
> Felix Holbrook
> Chester Joie

Source: From a printed leaflet quoted in A Documentary History of the Negro People in the United States. Vol. 1. Edited by Herbert Aptheker. New York: Citadel Press, 1951, pp. 7–8. In In Hope of Liberty: Culture, Community, and Protest Among Northern Free Blacks: 1700–1860, by James Oliver Horton and Lois E. Horton. New York: Oxford University Press, 1997.

colonial merchants and planters. Suddenly, the British government was spending considerable sums of money in the colonies to outfit ships and to feed and clothe soldiers. As demand for goods soared, so did the demand for labor, and people flocked from various parts of the world to live and work in the colonies.

Many of the poor laborers who journeyed to the New World to work for the newly rich had a hard time of it. Finding year-round work was not guaranteed, and much time was spent moving from city to city, looking for seasonal work. The men worked on the docks, loading and unloading trade ships when they were in port. They cut down and processed lumber, fished, and hunted whales. They also worked as wagon drivers, construction workers, tailors, and shoemakers.

Although America's resources were vast, they were not fairly distributed between the rich and the poor. During times of unemployment, the working poor dug for oysters or sought charity from religious relief agencies. Sometimes there were so many poor people seeking help, especially in the larger cities, that city officials declared them ineligible for assistance and ordered them out of town. The children of the poor were periodically removed from their families and forced to become apprentices to skilled tradespeople; this way, they could learn an occupation that would take them off the charitable lists.

Colonial population centers just before the Revolution

By 1760 Philadelphia, Pennsylvania, a port city, was the major point of entry for immigrants to the New World. It was by far the largest city in the colonies, with a population of about 18,000. The city had been settled in 1681 by Englishman William Penn (1644–1718), a Quaker (member of the Society of Friends, a Christian sect that promotes justice, peace, and simplicity in living).

During the 1760s fine new buildings were constructed in Philadelphia, including Carpenters Hall and the Old State House, where independence would be declared in 1776. People flocked to this sophisticated and cultured city, and many decided to stay; by 1774 the population had grown to 40,000, making Philadelphia the second-largest city in the British Empire next to London. Revolutionary-era heroes Benjamin Franklin (1706–1790) and Betsy Ross (1752–1836) called Philadelphia home.

New York, New York, another bustling port city, ranked second in 1774, with a population of between 25,000 and 30,000. It had been settled by the Dutch in 1624 but was surrendered to the English in 1664. The city would serve as British army headquarters throughout most of the Revolutionary War.

Boston, Massachusetts, was the third-largest city in the colonies on the eve of the Revolution. Settled by English clergyman William Blackstone (1723–1780) in the 1620s, Boston was a thriving port city, a center of learning, and home to great future Revolutionary leaders such as John Adams, Samuel Adams, and John Hancock. In 1774 Boston's population was 20,000.

Newport, Rhode Island, was the fourth-largest city in 1774, with a population of 12,000. It was settled in 1639 by people who had been expelled from (thrown out of) Massachusetts for their religious beliefs. Ignored by the other colonies because of this dispute over religion, Newport looked to the sea for its livelihood, and by 1690 it was one of North America's major ports. Some of the trade there was legal, but much was not. Pirates—those who robbed ships at sea—were a common sight in Newport. Throughout the 1760s the city served as a major slave-trading port for the British Empire.

English clergyman William Blackstone settled Boston, Massachusetts in the 1620s. *(Reproduced by permission of The Library of Congress.)*

In 1774, Charleston, South Carolina, ranked fifth in size in the colonies, with a population of about 10,000. It was named for King Charles II of England (1630–1685; reigned 1660–1685) and was first settled by people from England; by 1760 it was a thriving port city, home to people from the Caribbean Islands, French Protestants, Quakers, Scots, Irish, and Belgians. Charleston was known for its religious tolerance and its friendly relations with neighboring Native American tribes.

The first colonial settlers were undeniably hardy, spirited, and self-reliant. But the very qualities that contributed to the successful English settlement of eastern North America— the thirst for independence that fueled and defined colonial civilization—would later lead to troubled relations with the

Mother Country and, ultimately, a revolution for American independence.

For More Information

Books

Commager, Henry Steele, and Richard B. Morris, eds. *The Spirit of Seventy-Six: The Story of the American Revolution as Told by Participants*. Originally published in 1958. Reprinted. New York: Da Capo Press, 1995, pp. 1–9, 38–58.

Johnson, Paul. *A History of the American People*. New York: HarperCollins, 1997, pp. 121–77.

Web Sites

"American Revolution Timeline: Early Colonial Era." The History Place. [Online] Available http://www.historyplace.com/unitedstates/revolution/rev-early.htm (accessed on December 6, 1999).

"American Revolution Timeline: English Colonial Era." The History Place. [Online] Available http://www.historyplace.com/unitedstates/revolution/rev-col.htm (accessed on December 6, 1999).

"Liberty Perspectives." [Online] Available http://www0.pbs.org/ktca/liberty/perspectives/dailylife.html (accessed on December 6, 1999).

"The Story of the Pilgrims." [Online] Available http://www.plimoth.org/Library/pilgrim.htm (accessed on December 6, 1999).

Additional links can be accessed through "Yahooligans! Around the World: Countries: United States: History: Colonial Life (1585–1783): American Revolutionary War." [Online] Available http://www.yahooligans.com/Around_the_World/... (accessed on April 16, 1999).

Sources

Allison, Robert J. *American Eras: The Revolutionary Era*. Detroit: Gale, 1998.

Dolan, Edward F. *The American Revolution: How We Fought the War of Independence*. Brookfield, CT: Millbrook Press, 1995.

Horton, James Oliver and Lois E. Horton. *In Hope of Liberty: Culture, Community, and Protest Among Northern Free Blacks: 1700–1860*. New York: Oxford University Press, 1997.

Jones, Jacqueline. "Race, Sex, and Self-Evident Truths: The Status of Slave Women during the Era of the American Revolution." In *Women in the Age of the American Revolution*. Ronald Hoffman and Peter J. Albert, eds. Charlottesville: University Press of Virginia, 1989, pp. 293–337.

Lecky, William E. Hartpole. *History of England in the Eighteenth Century.* 7 vols. New York: AMS Press, 1968. Vol. 3, p. 379.

Lloyd, Alan. *The King Who Lost America: A Portrait of the Life and Times of George III.* Garden City, NY: Doubleday, 1971, pp. 190–91.

Miller, John C. *Origins of the American Revolution.* Stanford, CA: Stanford University Press, 1959.

Schouler, James. *Americans of 1776: Daily Life during the Revolutionary Period.* Williamstown, MA: Corner House, 1984.

Colonial Life

Up until the second half of the seventeenth century, the British government was far too preoccupied with its own problems to closely monitor and regulate colonial policy. So, in virtually every aspect of daily life, from providing their families with food and shelter to establishing schools and churches to organizing recreational activities, the New World settlers had to start from scratch. By the time of the American Revolution, the English colonists had turned the North American wilderness into a structured, mainly agricultural, and highly literate society—a society that was built on ingenuity and thrived on autonomy (the right to direct its own affairs).

What did people eat before the Revolution?

The diet of colonial Americans varied, depending on the food at hand and the origins of the people who lived in a given area. Some foods, however, were considered staple items (basics that everyone consumed). In 1763, 90 percent of all Americans were farmers, so the hardiest vegetables—those that

This reconstruction of a colonial Christmas breakfast includes a molded loaf with meat and onion, wrapped in greens. *(Reproduced by permission of Corbis Corporation [Bellevue].)*

were easy to grow and could be stored for long periods of time without rotting—appeared on most colonial tables. These included beans, potatoes, sweet potatoes, and turnips. Since settlements tended to grow up along the ocean or rivers, seafood was often on the menu. Oysters were popular with nearly everyone, but—very surprisingly—lobsters were considered fit only for the poor.

New York, New Jersey, and especially Pennsylvania were considered the colonial "breadbasket." Farmers there grew wheat to supply the colonies, Canada, and the West Indies. The green vegetables and the cheeses, salads, and apples introduced by the Germans and the Dutch made the diet in these colonies more varied than in any other part of the New World.

The Scots-Irish in Pennsylvania and the Southern backcountry depended on hunting and fishing, often using techniques they learned from Native Americans. They lived mostly on wild fruits and greens, bear, venison (deer meat), rabbit, squirrel, woodchuck, and turkey. These people moved frequently, so they did little serious farming. Occasionally, though, they would clear a small patch of land to grow sweet potatoes, turnips, corn, beans, or squash.

Pork was popular in New England (Massachusetts, Rhode Island, New Hampshire, Connecticut, and Vermont). Pigs were easy to raise almost anywhere—they could forage for food in wooded areas or even on city streets. A man called a "hog-reeve" was often hired to keep these ill-tempered beasts under control. The New England diet was frequently rounded out with white bread, milk porridge, and pumpkin that was roasted, boiled, mashed, and then made into bread, cakes, and pies.

Some Southern farmers cultivated great quantities of rice. Milk was popular in the South, as elsewhere, but it could not be kept fresh in the warmer Southern colonies, so it was not a staple item there. The diet of the poor Southerner might include only three or four ingredients, but wealthy Southerners fared better. Harriot Horry, who was the daughter of a wealthy South Carolina planter, compiled a cookbook in 1770. It includes directions for the preparation of beef, veal, seafood dishes, Shrewsbury cakes (shortbread cookies made with sugar, butter, nutmeg, and flour), cheesecakes, marmalades, gingerbread, almond cream, and strawberry jellies.

Literacy in the colonies

The written word was just as powerful a force for freedom before the Revolutionary War as weapons were during the war. Americans were an uncommonly literate group of people (able to read and write). The founders of the colonies feared that their distance from civilization would turn the population into savages. Early settlers in the New England area were especially concerned about their children's future: they combined elements of Christian education with reading and literacy by using the Bible as an early reading text.

How many Americans were able to read? Estimates vary, but historians agree that by the time of the Revolution, the percentage of the population that could read was far higher in America than in Europe. It is harder to estimate how many African Americans could read, but there is evidence that a fair number could, especially those living in the North.

As early as 1642, Massachusetts parents who failed to teach their children to read were fined. As communities grew, New Englanders established extensive public schools. The goal of these schools was to teach every colonist to read. In Massachusetts, Connecticut, and New Hampshire, children benefitted from more and better educational facilities than those in any other part of America.

Although public education in the other colonies was less equitable, most white colonists—both male and female— could read. Most also owned at least a few books, often the Bible and an almanac (a book containing lists, charts, and tables of useful information).

Fueling independent thought

On the eve of the Revolution, the colonists were a literate and independent-minded people. American colonists apparently loved to read and write and were deeply interested in following the news and arguments of the day. Newspapers played an especially important role in the colonists' lives. They were read eagerly, with people sharing their copies and discussing the headlines. With such a large reading population, it was no wonder that many colonists were opposed to the Stamp Act (see Chapter 4: The Roots of Rebellion [1763–1769]), which taxed the very paper upon which their newspapers, pamphlets, and books were printed.

While most early Americans could and did read, highly educated people read more widely. At this point in U.S. history, it was not considered necessary for young women to attend institutions of higher learning, but young men studied the classics in American colleges—usually in the original Latin and Greek. They also read the works of European philosophers of their day (philosophy is the study of the nature of things, based on logical reasoning). These studies proved to be a provocative mixture: they encouraged the patriots (freedom-fighters) to base the colonies' rebellion on principles of liberty, philosophy, and justice, not simply on economic matters like taxes.

For many colonial families, the fireplace served as the gathering place after the evening meal. Here a man enjoys his pipe and a woman knits while children play at her feet. *(Reproduced by permission of The Granger Collection, New York.)*

Education and the sexes

There were few opportunities for formal education for women prior to the American Revolution. Their education centered instead on managing a household and raising children. Even though women were the undisputed backbone of the American family unit, for most of the colonial era they were afforded no legal status whatsoever.

An example of a colonial schoolroom. Children of varying ages gathered in one large schoolroom, but were often separated into groups. *(Reproduced by permission of Corbis Corporation [Bellevue].)*

The number of skills colonial women had to master to perform their various roles was astonishing. They made their family's clothing from cloth they produced themselves. They also cooked, processed, and preserved food from crops they grew and tended; treated the sick with a variety of herbs; assisted in childbirth; took care of farm animals; educated young children; and assisted in the family business.

Women learned these skills from their mothers or served as apprentices or servants to other families. Girls and boys went to "dame schools" (taught by women known as dames) up to about the age of seven to learn how to read and write. Some girls were fortunate enough to receive a secondary education with the boys after dame school, or they were tutored at home or went to private schools.

Educational opportunities for women varied from colony to colony. Until about 1750 in New England, for instance, education for girls usually stopped after dame school;

Harvard College was the choice of many colonial-era men looking to further their education. Some women were fortunate enough to receive a secondary education after "dame school," but for most women, their education never progressed to the college level. *(Reproduced by permission of Corbis Corporation [Bellevue].)*

later, however, many girls attended "town schools" just like the boys. Boys and girls were educated separately, though—the girls had their turn in the summer or at the end of the day after the boys' classes were over. The quality of the education at town schools was said to be better for boys. The first all-female town school opened in Portsmouth, New Hampshire, in 1773, for the teaching of reading, writing, arithmetic, and geography. Girls who sought further education could attend a handful of private schools—if their families could afford the tuition.

Educational prospects were better for girls in New York, Pennsylvania, and New Jersey than they were for the girls in the rest of the Northeast. Even though they too were expected to devote their lives to family and household, they were fortunate to receive an elementary education equal to that of boys in schools operated by the Dutch Reformed Church, Quakers, and various German religious groups like the Moravians. Moravians believed girls had the same ability to learn as boys: they established schools for both sexes, as well as some all-girl schools.

Revolutionary-Era Colleges

Colonial colleges were very small. In 1775 there were nine colleges with a total of 750 students. Eight of the nine were associated with the religious groups who had founded them. It was very costly to attend college, so a college education was limited for the most part to the male children of the wealthy. Many of the Founding Fathers—leaders in the movement to establish a free and independent United States—received law degrees from one of these institutions. An English visitor to the colonies once complained that it seemed as though every other American he met was a lawyer.

The following is a list of American colleges that could grant degrees during the American Revolution. Four other colleges were added in 1782–1783.

Original Name	Modern Name
Harvard College (founded 1636)	Harvard University (Massachusetts)
College of William and Mary	College of William and Mary (Virginia)
Yale College	Yale University (Connecticut)
College of New Jersey	Princeton University (New Jersey)
Kings College	Columbia University (New York)
College of Philadelphia	University of Pennsylvania
College of Rhode Island	Brown University
Queens College	Rutgers University (New Jersey)
Dartmouth College	Dartmouth College (New Hampshire)

Sources: Beverly McAnear, "College Founding in the American Colonies, 1745–1775," Mississippi Valley Historical Review, 42 (1955): 24–44; David W. Robson, "College Founding in the New Republic, 1776–1800," History of Education Quarterly, 23 (1983): 323. In Robert J. Allison, American Eras: The Revolutionary Era, 1754–1783. Detroit: Gale, 1998, pp. 132–34.

The leading pre-Revolutionary girls' school was founded in 1754 in Philadelphia; female students there studied reading, writing, arithmetic, and English grammar. A girls' boarding school was opened in Philadelphia in 1767. Private and evening schools were also options.

A high quality education for girls was more difficult to obtain in the South, partly because of the region's geography. Large, scattered farms and plantations made a town-school system impractical. Fewer Southern girls were able to read and write, and education was considered a private family affair.

Young children were taught by their mothers; later, tutors were hired. Tutors might instruct a boy's sisters in domestic matters, music, dancing, art, needlework, conduct, good manners, and possibly conversational French. Poor girls might become apprentices and learn how to read the Bible and perform household tasks; some attended the few free schools available, but most poor children received no education at all.

The sporting life

Because the American continent was fertile, the early settlers did not have to spend all of their time finding and growing food. Colonial Americans, therefore, had a fair amount of free time for sports and recreation. They enjoyed the European games and sports they had brought with them (cards, lawn bowling, and dancing) and embraced the Native American pastime of gambling. People bet heavily on the outcomes of sporting events, horse races, fistfights, and card games. In 1765 William Byrd, one of the richest men in the colonies, reportedly had to sell 400 slaves to pay off his gambling debts.

Founding Father John Adams wrote in his *John Adams: A Biography in His Own Words:* "I spent my time driving hoops, playing marbles, playing Quoits [a game in which flat rings of iron or rope are pitched at a stake, with points awarded for encircling it], Wrestling, Swimming, Skaiting and above all in shooting." By the mid-1700s, activities that had once been necessary for survival had become recreational in nature. Many colonists spent their leisure time engaging in shooting contests, hunting, and fishing.

Beginning around 1730, wealthy men began to import racehorses from Great Britain. While British races were run on long, straight tracks, American colonists built oval tracks because the crowds of spectators were so large. Entire communities often attended the horse races, and the racing season might extend from March to November, depending on the local weather. In the mild climate of South Carolina, horse racing became such a part of everyday life that by 1763 newspapers were publishing the daily race results.

Rich and poor alike enjoyed unusual "sports" like bear baiting and cock fighting, both of which are considered cruel,

violent, and abusive in present-day society. Although bear baiting had been outlawed in Massachusetts in 1631, that did not stop its practice. Bear baiting involves setting dogs to attack or torment a chained bear. Cock fighting takes place between two game birds (game cocks) that sometimes have metal spurs attached to their legs to make the fight bloodier. Special pits were built for cock fights, usually in taverns, with a raised area for spectators, who, of course, gambled heavily on the results.

Boxing in the colonies was not the refined sport it was in England. In his book *American Eras: The Revolutionary Era (1754-1783)* Robert J. Allison describes how the American version of this sport differed from the British version. According to Allison, American boxing fans gathered at taverns to watch matches between two men whose object was to gouge one another in the genitals with waxed fingernails grown especially for the purpose.

Many colonial boys and girls learned how to dance through the instruction of a tutor. Such lessons often came in handy at colonial weddings and parties.
(Source unknown.)

Taverns hosted shooting matches, lawn bowling tournaments, and meetings to discuss politics. Boston's most skilled political agitator, Samuel Adams (1722–1803; see section titled "The Sons of Liberty Unite" in Chapter 4: The Roots of Rebellion [1763–1769]), liked to stir up resistance to England through rousing speeches he delivered to local tavern crowds.

The most popular card game of the day was whist, a game that required bluffing one's opponents. The Germans called it *pochen* (to bluff), the French called it *poque,* and it came to be called *poker* by Americans. The Stamp Act of 1765 placed a tax on playing cards; that may have been the most unpopular feature of the Act.

Colonial settlements grew up around water sources, and water sports were popular pastimes. New England and Maryland colonists liked to race sailboats, rowboats, and canoes. Wealthy South Carolina planters escaped the summer heat by traveling to Rhode Island, where they enjoyed the pleasures of sailing. New Yorkers raced yachts, a Dutch invention (the word *yacht* comes from a Dutch word for hunting boat). Many Americans liked to swim; Founding Father Benjamin Franklin (1706–1790) liked it so much, he is said to have considered paying his way through Europe by becoming a swimming instructor.

American colonists did not share the British passion for football or cricket. Instead, they developed other European sports that placed an emphasis on individual skills. As early as 1762, colonists were playing a sport that resembled modern-day baseball. Soldiers under the command of George Washington (1732–1799) at Valley Forge, Pennsylvania, were reported in 1778 to be "playing at base." And so, along with hot dogs and apple pie, baseball would later come to be identified as something purely American.

For More Information
Books

Reich, Jerome R. *Colonial America.* 3rd ed. Englewood Cliffs, NJ: Prentice Hall, 1994.

Web Sites

Related web links can be accessed through "Yahooligans! Around the

World: Countries: United States: History: Colonial Life (1585–1783): American Revolutionary War." [Online] Available http://www. yahooligans.com/Around_the_World/... (accessed on April 16, 1999).

Sources

Adams, John. *John Adams: A Biography in His Own Words.* Edited by James Bishop Peabody. New York: Newsweek, 1973.

Allison, Robert J. *American Eras: The Revolutionary Era (1754-1783).* Detroit: Gale, 1998.

Ellet, Elizabeth. *Revolutionary Women in the War for American Independence.* A one-volume revised edition of the 1848 Landmark Series, edited and annotated by Lincoln Diamant. Westport, CT: Praeger, 1998.

Hoffman, Ronald, and Peter J. Albert, eds. *Women in the Age of the American Revolution.* Charlottesville: University Press of Virginia, 1989.

Lecky, William E. Hartpole. *History of England in the Eighteenth Century.* Vol. 3. New York: AMS Press, 1968.

Marrin, Albert. *The War for Independence: The Story of the American Revolution.* New York: Atheneum, 1988.

Schouler, James. *Americans of 1776: Daily Life during the Revolutionary Period.* Williamstown, MA: Corner House, 1984.

Literature and the Arts in the Revolutionary Era

By the time of the American Revolution (1775–83), American writers had ventured beyond the Puritan literary style and its religious themes and had developed styles of writing that grew from distinctly American experiences. (The Puritans were a group of Protestants who broke with the Church of England; they believed that church rituals should be simplified and that people should follow strict religious discipline.) The colonial fascination with science, nature, freedom, and innovation came through in the writings of the Revolutionary period. The colonists developed their own way of speaking as well, no longer copying the more formal style of British writers. (Noah Webster's *Blue-Backed Speller,* published in 1783, helped to standardize the new American version of English.)

Author David Hawke offered an example of the American literary style in *The Colonial Experience.* Founding Father Benjamin Franklin (1706–1790), he noted, "took the seventeenth-century saying 'Three may keep counsel, if two be away' and converted it into 'Three may keep a secret, if two of them are dead.'"

Some of the best literature of the colonial era described everyday life in New England and, in the process, depicted aspects of the fledgling American character. The colonists who would form a new nation were firm believers in the power of reason; they were ambitious, inquisitive, optimistic, practical, politically astute, and self-reliant.

What colonial children read

Up until about twenty-five years before the Revolutionary War began, the reading material for American children was restricted basically to the Bible and other religious works. Gradually, additional books were published and read more widely. Rivaling the Bible in popularity were almanacs. Children loved to read them for the stories, weather forecasts, poetry, news events, advice, and other assorted and useful information they contained. The most famous of these was Benjamin Franklin's *Poor Richard's Almanack,* first published in 1732. Franklin (see box titled "The Many Sides of Benjamin Franklin") claimed to have written *Poor Richard* because his wife could not bear to see him "do nothing but gaze at the Stars; and has threatened more than once to burn all my Books … if I do not make some profitable Use of them for the good of my Family." We have *Poor Richard* to thank for such lasting sayings as: "Eat to live, and not live to eat"; "He that lies down with Dogs, shall rise up with fleas"; "Little strokes fell big oaks"; and "Early to bed and early to rise/Makes a man healthy, wealthy, and wise."

All the American colonies had printing presses by 1760, but Americans and their children continued to rely on England as the source for most of their books. A London publisher by the name of John Newberry (1713–1767) is said to have had the greatest influence on children's literature in pre-Revolutionary America. He began publishing children's books in the 1740s. Most of them were educational, with titles such as *A Museum for Young Gentlemen and Ladies or A private tutor for little Masters and Misses* (1750; a how-to book on proper behavior) and *The Pretty Book for Children* (1750; a guide to the English language).

Books were quite expensive in the 1700s, though, so children usually advanced from the Bible and religious verses straight to adult-type literature. Especially popular in that category were storybooks such as *Robinson Crusoe* and *Arabian Nights*.

Prior to the Revolution, schoolbooks were imported from England and were available only to the wealthy. These books stressed self-improvement through hard work and careful spending. Such qualities, it was believed, could lead to wealth, which was the lesson learned in the popular storybook *Goody Two-Shoes: The Means by which she acquired her Learning and Wisdom, and in consequence thereof her Estate* [everything she owned] (1765). Goody Two-Shoes was a girl named Margery Meanwell, an orphan who was thrilled to receive two shoes to replace her one. She rose from humble beginnings, learning to read and later becoming a teacher; she went on to marry a wealthy man and matured into a "Lady" and a generous person.

The role of satire in the Revolutionary era

Up until the Revolutionary era, the Puritans who had settled New England had a profound influence on what was printed in the colonies: nearly all publications centered on a religious topic of some sort. The Puritans frowned on dramatic performances, as well. But by the mid-1700s, the Puritan influence was fading. In 1749 the first American acting troupe was established in Philadelphia. Seventeen years later, America's first permanent playhouse was built in the same city; in 1767 the Southwark Theatre staged the first play written by a native-born American, Thomas Godfrey's (1736–1763) *Prince of Parthia*.

By the mid-1760s, political writings by colonists were increasingly common and more and more forceful in nature. James Otis (1725–1783), a lawyer from Boston, published *The Rights of British Colonists Asserted and Proved* in 1764. And the hated Stamp Act, a tax law passed by the British in 1765 (see Chapter 4: The Roots of Rebellion [1763–1769]), prompted an even greater outpouring of writing of a political nature. (Parliament, England's lawmaking body, passed the Stamp Act to raise money from the colonies without receiving the consent of the colonial assemblies, or representatives.)

One of the most popular forms of political writing was satire, especially plays, essays, and poems. Satire pokes fun at human vices and foolishness. While most satiric works were written by men, some of the best-known plays of the day were written by a woman named Mercy Otis Warren (1728–1814).

Warren was the sister and wife of two patriots (James Otis and James Warren, respectively) and an eager participant in the political meetings held so often at her home. She was strategically placed in Boston to follow the events leading up to the American Revolution. Her first political drama, *The Adulateur,* was published anonymously (without her name) in Boston in 1773, soon after the shocking publication of Governor Thomas Hutchinson's (1711–1780) letters revealing his anti-patriot views (see Chapter 4: The Roots of Rebellion [1763–1769]). Not surprisingly, Warren's gift for satire was directed at pro-British leaders. The play's last words are spoken by a character based on Warren's brother, James Otis. Although he foresees war, he also predicts fame, victory, and eternal prosperity for the party of liberty.

During the war, Warren wrote several other dramatic satires that actively promoted the revolutionary cause, but her plays were never performed on stage. They were read by many people, though, and were performed privately for Warren's family and friends, including prominent Revolutionary figures such as Samuel, John, and Abigail Adams (see Chapter 4: The Roots of Rebellion [1763–1769].)

Other notable satirists put the war on stage. John Leacock's play *The Fall of British Tyranny,* which was performed in 1776, portrayed the notorious Battle of Bunker Hill (see Chapter 6: Lexington, Concord, and the Organization of Colonial Resistance) and the military discussions of American war leader George Washington. In plays by Warren and Leacock, Americans appeared as mythical or real figures from Greek and Roman days. In Warren's *Adulateur,* for example, the characters inspired by James Otis and his friend Samuel Adams are renamed Brutus and Cassius (early Roman political leaders). Audiences enjoyed the game of identifying the dramatists' thinly disguised portraits of public figures.

Benjamin Franklin, who seemed to be able to do anything, produced a long stream of political satires making fun of British policies. In his 1773 *Edict by the King of Prussia,* for

The Many Sides of Benjamin Franklin

American printer, politician, inventor, and writer Benjamin Franklin (1706–1790) hailed from an extremely large lower-middle-class family. (He was one of 17 children.) Because the Franklin family had only enough money to get by, young Ben received just two years of formal schooling. But hard work and success early in life allowed him time later on to devote to scientific experiments, political affairs, and public service. He is even credited with establishing America's first circulating library.

In 1729 Franklin bought the struggling *Pennsylvania Gazette* (later called the *Saturday Evening Post*) and transformed it into a profitable publication. While pursuing daring new scientific research—in 1751 he published *New Experiments and Observations on Electricity*—Franklin became involved in colonial politics, first as a member of the Pennsylvania Assembly and later as America's spokesperson in England. He is

Engraving of Benjamin Franklin, 1771, by H. Wright Smith. *(Reproduced by permission of Archive Photos, Inc.)*

remembered as a key leader in the fight for American rights. As early as 1754 Franklin had outlined his *Plan of the Union,* charting the course for colonial unity and independence from Great Britain. He later served as a member of the committee that drafted the Declaration of Independence.

example, he drew parallels between the settlement of England in the fifth century by Germans (then called Prussians) and the settlement of America. His intention was to show how ridiculous it was for Great Britain to think that just because she had settled America, she had the right to lay heavy taxes on her subjects. (The British held just the opposite view.) In the *Edict,* the King of Prussia makes the same trade and tax demands on the former German colonists in England that England was making on the American colonies in the 1760s and 1770s.

American lawyer and poet John Trumbull's (1750–1831) epic poem "M'Fingal," first published in 1776, became the most popular satirical poem of the American Revolution. The silly hero, M'Fingal, is a clownish Loyalist who argues at a town meeting that tyranny (unjust, severe, and often cruel rule) is justice. He is bested in this battle of words by the patriot Honorius, a character apparently based on American statesman (and, later, U.S. president) John Adams.

Poetry and popular songs of the Revolutionary era

As was true of most American arts before the Revolution, the Puritan influence on music was strong. The first songbook published in the colonies was the 1640 edition of the *Bay Psalm Book.* (Psalms [pronounced SOMS] are religious songs.) Another popular type of American music was the tavern song. Both psalms and tavern songs were forms of "community singing."

By the time of the Revolution, music in the colonies had not changed very much. Bostonian William Billings (1746–1800), who was the first important American composer, published six books of music, much of it original, including instructions on styles of singing to make it more lively. Billings mixed the serious with the humorous. His religious song "Chester" was so popular that he rewrote the words during the Revolution, transforming it into a warlike version called "Let Tyrants Shake."

Revolutionary-era songwriters wrote to inspire their listeners. Songs about the events of the day were especially popular because everyone—even those who could not read or write—could join in. American poet and wit Joel Barlow (1754–1812) wrote: "One good song is worth a dozen addresses or proclamations." Some patriotic songs were written by established writers of serious works. For example, John Dickinson (1732–1808), author of *Letters from a Farmer in Pennsylvania to Inhabitants of the British Colonies,* also wrote the popular "Liberty Song." But most songs seemed to come out of nowhere as anonymous or cooperative productions, evolving as people added to and altered the verses. Some of these songs have survived to the present-day, among them the ever-popular "Yankee Doodle." Originally a derogatory (DUR-oga-tore-ee; negative and belittling) ditty sung by the British (it depicted New Englanders as fools), this folk song later became the battle cry of the colonial forces.

Poetic expressions of patriotism were popular as well. Philip Freneau (1752–1832) produced so many well-written and stirring patriotic poems that he became known as the Poet of the American Revolution. Freneau became the new country's first lyric poet; that is, he wrote in a new, more personal, and more emotional style than had ever been known before.

One of the best-known Revolutionary-era poets was Phillis Wheatley (1753–1784), an African American slave from Boston. Her poems, which were even more successful in England than in the colonies, ranged from those on Christian topics, to translations of the Latin poet Ovid, to patriotic odes (poems designed for singing). She was so popular that one of her patriotic verses added to the vocabulary of the Revolution: in her 1775 poem to General Washington, she coined the usage of "Columbia" to refer to the new United States.

The role of wartime literature

Words may have been just as important as weapons in the Revolutionary cause. Patriotic writings came in many varieties. Some were crude efforts designed to sway public opinion to a cause, others were well-reasoned political arguments, and some were collections of inspirational verse.

In 1776 English-born political writer Thomas Paine (1737–1809) published a pamphlet titled *Common Sense*. This immensely popular work called for equality, freedom, and complete separation from Britain. According to Paine, the move toward independence was pure "common sense." Albert Marrin commented in *The War for Independence: The Story of the American Revolution*, "Tom Paine did more than anyone to change American minds in favor of independence.... *Common Sense* had the right ideas at the right time and became the first American bestseller.... Paine lit a fire that leaped across America."

Well before the release of Paine's *Common Sense*, other writers put forward arguments that paved the way toward independence. John Dickinson (1732–1808), author of the

John Dickinson wrote the "Olive Branch Petition" as a request for legal justice for Americans in matters of taxation and representation.
(Reproduced by permission of Archive Photos, Inc.)

"Olive Branch Petition," did not ask for independence from England as much as for legal justice for Americans in matters of taxation and representation. The character he portrayed—the gentleman farmer—was convincing because it represented many American ideals: industry (hard work), honesty, frugality (conserving; not being wasteful), education, and common sense.

As the war progressed, firsthand accounts of the fighting seized people's attention and kept them firm in their goal of defeating the British. Revolutionary soldier Ethan Allen (1738-1789) of Vermont wrote about his experiences as a prisoner of war. His wartime book, *A Narrative of Colonel Ethan Allen's Captivity* (1779), praised the courage of his Green Mountain Boys (an irregular army unit) and condemned the British. General Washington believed the book helped keep the Revolutionary cause alive during a particularly critical period in the war. Allen was famous before he wrote his book, but many ordinary people—women as well as men—also wrote about their Revolutionary War experiences.

By the end of the war, American writers were firmly established as important contributors to a uniquely American national identity—an identity separate from the colonists' European roots. Many of the writers who rose to prominence during the Revolution became even more famous after it was over. Mercy Otis Warren wrote a three-volume *History of the Rise, Progress, and Termination of the American Revolution* (1805), which appeared under her own name—a remarkable accomplishment in an era dominated by male writers.

The role of the press in colonial America

The earliest American newspaper on record was published in the South in 1638. By the time of the American Revolution, there were forty–two newspapers being printed in the colonies, with the New England, Middle, and Southern colonies represented evenly. About a third of the newspapers were Loyalist in tone (they favored the preservation of colonial ties to Britain). The majority of the colonial newspapers were issued weekly and were purchased by subscription by several hundred people. But many more colonists actually *heard* the news, which was read aloud in taverns.

Sharing the news by reading it aloud in public places served two purposes: 1) it made the news available to those unable to pay for a paper, and 2) it informed people of current events even if they were unable to read. (At the time of the American Revolution, almost half the male population was illiterate.)

Colonial newspapers provided different information than modern papers do. A typical colonial paper, sometimes called a broadsheet or broadside, was four pages long (a large sheet folded in half and printed as four pages). The front page was filled with advertisements. The other pages carried reprints of news stories from other papers and the text of speeches and sermons. The papers also offered poetry, letters, essays, and editorials (statements of opinions). Many editorials were unsigned so that the authorities could not find and punish the colonial authors who urged the colonists to rebel against English rule.

In colonial America prior to 1775, information was shared by people traveling by horseback, on foot, or by ship. News arrived slowly and was eagerly awaited. The newspapers were one way for patriots to share their messages of the benefits of declaring the American colonies' independence from England. At this point in time, each colony considered itself a separate entity. By showing the colonists that they had something in common (their grievances against England), the

Loyalist Writers during the Revolutionary Era

Not all colonists supported the war effort; many wanted to maintain political ties with Britain. Their "Loyalist" philosophy was represented in the works of poets Jonathan Odell (1737–1818) and Joseph Stansbury. Loyalists' writings and their mixed feelings about American independence lasted throughout the war and beyond. Jonathan Boucher (1738–1804), an English clergyman and Loyalist writer who spent sixteen years in the colonies, fled to England in 1775. After the war he wrote a Loyalist interpretation of the conflict, *A View of the Causes and Consequences of the American Revolution* (1797). Although he disagreed with the patriot cause, he admired its leader and dedicated his book to George Washington.

The artist Gilbert Stuart's image was captured in this painting, titled "Gilbert Stuart," by artist John Neagle. *(Reproduced by permission of Corbis Corporation [Bellevue].)*

newspapers helped forge a sense of community among the colonies. This feeling of unity—of being one nation—was vital to the colonies' success in gaining their freedom from England.

Arts of the Revolutionary era

Before about 1750, wealthy Americans imported most of their artworks and home furnishings from England. As more and more artisans (crafters) arrived in the New World, they began to produce goods that rivaled the best England could turn out. Other American artists admired the sophisticated styles of Europe, but they were comfortable with a range of tastes and styles. Boston patriot Paul Revere (1735–1818), for example, made everything from fine silver and pewter bowls to a set of false teeth for General Washington.

The early eighteenth century brought European painters to the colonies. They pleased their wealthy customers by imitating successful European styles, often producing portraits of rich colonials posed as they might have been in an English portrait. A rich man who had earned his money in trade, for instance, might be depicted standing at a window gazing out at a ship.

As the century progressed, young American artists began to paint in a new way. Artists like Benjamin West (1738–1820), Gilbert Stuart (1755–1828), Charles Willson Peale (1741–1827), and John Singleton Copley (1738–1815) represented the finest in American artistic achievement. Their subjects were portrayed in the act of pursuing everyday endeavors. Copley depicted patriot John Adams standing with a document in one hand and pointing at another on his desk, apparently in the middle of writing a speech. Likewise, he portrayed Paul Revere in his work clothes, sitting at his work table near a teapot he had made.

The arts developed slowly in the New World. John Adams believed that this was the way it should be, because there was more important and practical work to be done first. In *John Adams: A Biography in His Own Words,* Adams declared: "I must study politics and war, that my sons may have liberty to study mathematics and philosophy, geography, natural history, and naval architecture, navigation, commerce, and agriculture, in order to give their children a right to study painting, poetry, music, architecture, statuary, tapestry and porcelain."

**"President John Adams,"
painting by John Singleton
Copley.** *(Reproduced by
permission of Corbis
Corporation [Bellevue].)*

For More Information
Books

Adams, John. *John Adams: A Biography in His Own Words.* Edited by James Bishop Peabody. New York: Newsweek, 1973.

Allison, Robert J. *American Eras: The Revolutionary Era (1754-1783).* Detroit: Gale, 1998.

Becker, Carl L. *Benjamin Franklin.* Ithaca, NY: Cornell University Press, 1946.

Bowen, Catherine Drinker. *The Most Dangerous Man in America: Scenes from the Life of Benjamin Franklin.* Boston: Little, Brown, 1974.

Emerson, Everett, ed. *Major Writers of Early American Literature.* Madison: University of Wisconsin Press, 1972.

Fleming, Thomas. *The Man Who Dared the Lightning: A New Look at Benjamin Franklin.* New York: William Morrow, 1970.

Franklin, Benjamin. *Benjamin Franklin's Autobiography.* Edited by J. A. Leo Lemay and P. M. Zall. New York: Norton, 1986.

Nye, Russell B. *The Cultural Life of the New Nation, 1776–1830.* New York: Harper, 1960.

Tyler, Moses C. *The Literary History of the American Revolution: 1763–1863.* New York: F. Ungar, 1957.

Patience Wright, Sculptor and Spy

The first known professional portrait sculptor in America was a woman. Patience Lovell Wright (1725–c. 1785) worked with wax, molding realistic busts (representations of a head, neck, and upper chest) as well as hands and faces. Sometimes her life-size hands and faces were attached to clothed figures. She turned to this line of work in 1769 after her husband died, leaving her with five children to support.

In the mid-1770s Wright moved to London, where her artistic skill and odd mannerisms (a loud voice and intense stare) attracted the attention of many important people. She listened to their gossip, and when the American Revolution began, she was able to pass on useful information to the American patriots. She sometimes hid messages in the wax heads she made of important British politicians, then sent the heads to her sister Rachel in Philadelphia, who forwarded the messages to General Washington.

Source: Wayne Craven, Sculpture in America. *New York: Crowell, 1968. See also "Wright, Patience Lovell" in* The Britannica Encyclopedia of American Art. *New York: Simon & Schuster, 1973, p. 610.*

Wright, Louis B. *The Cultural Life of the American Colonies, 1607–1763.* New York: Harper, 1957.

Web Sites

Campbell, D. *Brief Timeline of American Literature and Events: Pre-1620 to 1920.* [Online] Available http://www.gonzaga.edu/faculty/campbell/enl311/timefram.htm (accessed on December 6, 1999).

Sources
Books

Avery, Gillian. *Behold the Child: American Children and Their Books, 1621–1922.* Baltimore, MD: Johns Hopkins University Press, 1994.

Commager, Henry Steele, and Richard B. Morris, eds. *The Spirit of Seventy-Six: The Story of the American Revolution as Told by Participants.* New York: Da Capo Press, 1995, pp. 892–911.

Franklin, Benjamin. *Poor Richard's Almanack, 1733-1758.* In *Benjamin Franklin: Writings.* New York: Library of America, 1987, pp. 1181–1304.

Hawke, David. *The Colonial Experience.* Indianapolis, IN: Bobbs-Merrill, 1966.

Johnson, Paul. "The Role of Benjamin Franklin." In *A History of the American People.* New York: HarperCollins, 1997.

Web Sites

"Franklin, Benjamin." *DISCovering U. S. History.* [Online] Available (password required) http://www.galenet.com (accessed on January 25, 2000).

Reuben, Paul P. "Chapter 2: Colonial Period: 1700–1800—An Introduction." *PAL: Perspectives in American Literature—A Research and Reference Guide.* [Online] Available http://www.csustan.edu/english/reuben/pal/chap2/2intro.html (accessed on December 6, 1999).

The Roots of Rebellion (1763–1769)

4

With the French defeated at the close of the Seven Years' War (1756–63), Great Britain had new problems—far greater ones than she could handle. The war with France had resulted in the accumulation of many debts. The British were now in charge of a remote New World frontier that was populated by hostile Native American tribes. And no sooner had the French been expelled from North America than there was trouble with the Indians.

Native Americans had no great love for the British colonists. They had welcomed British settlers to the New World in the early 1600s, but gradually the land-hungry colonists pushed the Native tribes out of their homeland along the eastern seaboard. The displaced tribes, in turn, drove other tribes off their ancestral lands and into the southern Great Lakes area.

The Native Americans in the Great Lakes area enjoyed a peaceful relationship with the French who trapped furs there and traded European goods with them. Unwelcome changes came when British traders made their way to the region in the 1730s. The British had different ways of dealing with Native Americans. Unlike the French, they did not

After Pontiac's Rebellion, British Major Robert Rogers smoked a peace pipe with Chief Pontiac. When the colonists began to spread into Indian territory, relations between England and the Native Americans became strained.
(Reproduced by permission of Corbis Corporation [Bellevue].)

believe in cementing friendships by giving gifts. They were unwilling to hand over guns and ammunition to the Natives. In addition, British trappers and traders cheated the Indians out of their goods and land.

Pontiac's Rebellion

Finally, the Indians of the Ohio Valley became desperate. They knew it was only a matter of time before large numbers of English settlers would crowd into their territory. Indians of several tribes united under the leadership of Chief Pontiac (c. 1720–1769) of the Ottawa, a tribe known for its great warriors and hunters.

In Pontiac's Rebellion of 1763, the Indians captured British forts in a sweep across the western American frontier from New York to Virginia. Hundreds of pioneer families were killed. Hostilities continued to boil for years, but the rebellion

Native Americans Urged Not to Join the Fight

When it became clear that a war with Great Britain was likely, colonial governors grew increasingly concerned over the issue of Indian relations. The Native people had many grievances against the colonists: American settlers had trespassed on their land, and American traders had cheated them. The Indians had a more agreeable relationship with England, which in 1763 had promised to keep American colonists out of Native lands west of the Appalachian Mountains (see section titled "Proclamation of 1763").

At best, leaders of the colonial government hoped to get a pledge of neutrality (noninvolvement) from the Indian nations. Congress appointed commissioners to go out and deliver this speech to the Native American peoples:

Brothers and friends!... This is a family quarrel between us and Old England. You Indians are not concerned in it. We don't wish you to take up the hatchet against the king's troops. We desire you to remain at home, and not join on either side, but keep the hatchet buried deep.... Brothers, observe well! What is it we have asked of you? Nothing but peace ... and if application should be made to you by any of the king's unwise and wicked ministers to join on their side, we only advise you to deliberate [a verb; pronounced dih-LIB-uh-rate; think it over and discuss], with great caution, and in your wisdom look forward to the consequences of a compliance. For if the king's troops take away our property, and destroy us who are of the same blood as themselves, what can you, who are Indians, expect from them afterwards?

Source: James J. O'Donnell, III, Southern Indians in the American Revolution. *Knoxville: The University of Tennessee Press, 1973.*

was crushed within a matter of months—not by Americans but by British redcoat soldiers. According to Lee Sultzman, British military commander Simeon Ecuyer arranged to have smallpox-infected blankets delivered to the Indians. The terrible disease spread quickly, and, as a result, thousands of Native Americans and British colonists died. Through invasion and conquest, the whites would go on to claim and settle the rest of the present-day United States.

Proclamation of 1763

Great Britain was quick to point out that British soldiers—not Americans—were the ones who finally put down

Pontiac's Rebellion. Several pressing issues now confronted the British government: How were the Indians to be treated? In spite of the often bad relations between whites and Native Americans, the British believed that the Indians were entitled to certain rights as the original inhabitants of the New World land. How were these rights to be balanced against the wishes of American colonists? North American furs were highly prized in Great Britain, and skilled Indian hunters were vital to the fur trade. Should Native hunting grounds be reserved for Indians alone, or should whites be allowed to hunt there as well? How was the frontier to be made safe from land-grabbing Americans until a land policy could be worked out?

The British thought the time was right to tackle these issues, and King George III's (1738–1820; reigned 1760–1820) solution was the Proclamation of 1763. It laid down a boundary line along the Appalachian Mountains to separate the colonies from Indian land—land that the British considered barren and useless anyway, except for its prized furs. In the Proclamation of 1763, King George stated: "We do strictly forbid, on pain of our displeasure, all our loving subjects from making any purchases or settlements whatever in that region."

Any colonists who were already west of the line were ordered to move eastward. American colonists were to be confined to the eastern seaboard, where they could more easily be controlled by England, the so-called "Mother Country." King George also ordered that new forts be built on the frontier and be manned by British soldiers, who would direct and manage Indian affairs and keep the peace in the region. This was a costly proposal.

American reaction to English meddling

Ever since the settlement of the New World, the colonies had handled most of their own affairs without interference from England. "Being left alone became an indispensable component of the colonists' sense of well-being," wrote Bruce and William Catton in *The Bold and Magnificent Dream: America's Founding Years, 1492–1815.* "By the middle of the eighteenth century they had grown too accustomed, too strong, and too self-confident to submit to any other kind of handling." But now England had decided to meddle. Americans believed that unlimited westward expansion was both their right and their destiny. The colonists were incensed by the king's command to establish an Indian-controlled frontier. In retrospect, many critics note that the Proclamation of 1763 was not a very practical document: it would have been nearly impossible to enforce. An unknown number of settlers already lived west of the boundary line, and there would have been no way to move them, short of marching them out at gunpoint.

The Proclamation was just the first of a series of British acts to which American colonists would object over the next twelve years. As Americans asserted their rights as a free people within the British Empire, Britain insisted that they still had duties as loyal British subjects. Within twenty years, Great Britain—the world's foremost military power—would forever lose control of this spirited nation.

This is the Place to affix the STAMP.

The Stamp Act declared that as of November 1765, certain documents and other items ranging from newspapers to playing cards had to have stamps affixed to them. *(Reproduced by permission of The Library of Congress.)*

Stamp Act of 1765

English attempts to profit from the growth of American trade had begun back in 1651 with the passage of the Navigation Acts, which restricted trade and required that English ships be used to conduct colonial trade activity. More than a century later, the British government was intent on raising funds to pay off its war debts (equal to more than $30 billion in present-day currency, incurred during the French and Indian War) and pay for forts and soldiers in Indian territory. While the British had been financing the costly defense of the colonies against the French, many Americans prospered by providing for the needs of the fighting British soldiers. Other colonists had grown rich from smuggling (bringing goods in and taking them out of the country illegally, without paying taxes on them; see box titled "Did Smuggling Cause the Amer-

Did Smuggling Cause the American Revolution?

Some historians suggest that smuggling caused the American Revolution. Goods that are *smuggled* are brought into or taken out of a country without having legal duties (taxes) paid on them. It is true that smuggling by Americans was a common occurrence in the eighteenth century and a serious violation of British laws regulating trade in the colonies. The British charged high duties on items imported into the colonies in order to benefit British merchants and planters, but smugglers avoided these duties by bringing in cheaper goods produced by countries other than Great Britain.

Several acts were passed in the 1760s by a British government determined to stop American smugglers. British tax collectors, naval officers, royal governors, and other officials were put on alert to make sure taxes were collected and trade regulations observed. British ships patrolled the Atlantic Coast, stopping, searching, and holding ships suspected of smuggling goods. These actions put a severe crimp in the cherished American freedom to trade at will. After a particularly heated incident involving wealthy Boston merchant John Hancock and his boat *Liberty* in the spring of 1768, British soldiers were sent over to ensure peace in Boston. The presence of British troops only aggravated the situation further.

ican Revolution?"). Great Britain had been too busy with her world war to do anything about the smuggling. But after the war was over, the British government turned its attention to the war debt—and turned to the colonies for money to help offset it.

The Sugar Act and the Currency Act were passed by Parliament, England's lawmaking body, in 1764. The first increased taxes on sugar, coffee, wine, dye, and several other goods; the second prohibited the colonies from printing their own paper money. Both acts were clear attempts on the part of Great Britain to assert her power over the colonies. Their passage intensified the colonists' feelings of bitterness and resentment toward the Mother Country, further alienating the already disillusioned Americans. To raise even more money to cover the cost of sending British troops to the colonies, Parliament passed the extremely controversial Stamp Act in 1765. At the same time, the equally disturbing Quartering Act went into effect, requiring colonists to house and feed British troops. Americans were outraged.

The Stamp Act declared that as of November 1765, certain documents and other items ranging from newspapers to playing cards had to have stamps affixed (attached) to them. Unstamped documents were of no value. The stamps denoted payment of a "direct" tax to England, even though the colonists had no representatives in Parliament. Stamps had to be purchased from official Parliamentary-appointed stamp agents. Many prominent colonial men eagerly applied for this well-paying job—and then lived to regret it.

Parliament and King George thought the stamp tax was a rather small sacrifice to ask of the colonists, yet the services it would pay for (management of Indian territory, for instance) were enormous. American colonists were paying only a tiny fraction of the taxes that the English paid, and many colonists lived far more comfortably than the people of England. King George and Parliament, believing it was high time the colonies sent more money to England, were not prepared for the Americans' reactions to the Stamp Act.

Pamphlets and resolutions

Colonial opposition to the Stamp Act grew quickly. Newspaper articles, pamphlets, and lectures about "taxation without representation" (the colonies had no representatives in Parliament) fanned the flames of indignation. It was a bad time for Parliament to be trying to collect taxes. The colonies were suffering from a smallpox epidemic. On top of that, many people found themselves out of work at the end of the French and Indian War. Colonial lawmaking bodies up and down the East Coast, from Rhode Island to South Carolina, passed strongly worded resolutions against the Stamp Act. Insisting on their right to tax themselves, they declared that Britain seemed determined to enslave Americans. In Virginia, Representative Patrick Henry (1763–1799) spoke against the Stamp Act before the colony's lawmaking body, the House of Burgesses. His fellow representatives were speechless with admiration at his eloquent words, but newspapers in England

The passage of the Stamp Act in 1765 angered colonists, and they in turn rioted in the streets, protesting this taxation. *(Reproduced by permission of The Library of Congress.)*

wondered why he was not tossed in jail for treason (speaking out against his king). "If *this* be treason," contended Henry, "make the most of it."

After Henry's stirring words, the Virginia House passed a resolution declaring that the colony's General Assembly had "the only and sole exclusive right and power to lay taxes ... upon the inhabitants of this Colony." Anyone who said otherwise was viewed as an enemy of the colony. The Virginia resolution was a direct challenge to Parliament's authority.

"Howling mobs in the streets"

The unfortunate men who accepted jobs as stamp agents felt the anger of mobs (or possibly members of secret anti-British organizations like the Sons of Liberty; see "The Sons of Liberty Unite"), who destroyed their property and hanged or burned effigies (images or dummies of them) to show their contempt. Finally, the job became so dangerous that every stamp agent quit his post. In *The Reluctant Rebels*, author Lynn Montross described the disorder that grew from the passage of the Stamp Act this way: "Mobs of howling Liberty Boys surged through the streets of every town in America. There was a great deal of spectacular hell-raising, which reached a climax when forts occupied by British [soldiers] were attacked in New York and both Carolinas."

Nonimportation agreements

American resistance was not limited to words alone. A nonimportation policy was adopted, whereby colonial merchants refused to accept imported British goods. (This is known as a boycott.) Soon British merchants were crying out for the repeal of the Stamp Act. In the colonies, a Stamp Act Congress met in New York. Its members informed King George that colonial residents would not recognize or tolerate His Majesty's policy of taxation without representation.

The colonies did have some friends in Parliament who voiced their objections to the Stamp Act. High-ranking English politician William Pitt (1708–1778), sixty-seven years old and ailing, argued that the act should be done away with. "I rejoice that America has resisted!" he declared. "Were I but ten years younger I should spend the rest of my days in America, which has given the most brilliant proofs of its independent spirit."

The Sons of Liberty Unite

Long before the Stamp Act was passed by the British Parliament, the expressions "sons of freedom" and "sons of liberty" were used commonly by Americans whose parents or grandparents had fled to the New World to escape ill treatment in other lands. The phrase "sons of liberty" became even more popular in 1765. Parliament was discussing the proposal to tax the American colonists, and a pro-American British politician by the name of Isaac Barré spoke passionately against the proposal. Barré was a soldier who had fought in America and knew the country and its people well. He reminded Parliament that a people who had "fled tyranny [a harsh and unjust government] ... [and] exposed themselves to almost all the hardships to which human nature is liable" were not likely to put up with British oppression.

When the Stamp Act was passed in 1765 and Americans saw the danger it posed to their liberty, the name Sons of Liberty was gradually adopted by various groups throughout the colonies who opposed the act. Some of these groups were already meeting under other names such as the Charleston (South Carolina) Fire Company (volunteer firefighters) and the Loyal Nine, a Boston social club.

Samuel Adams was an active supporter of the Sons of Liberty and his writings inspired many colonists to rebel against King George. *(Source unknown.)*

The Sons exchanged letters with their brother organizations, keeping them informed on the progress of resistance to the Stamp Act. The letters—and the organizations—were supposed to be secret, but it was hard to maintain secrecy while trying to build up support among the population for the cause. The Sons claimed to oppose violence, but violence often erupted when large crowds gathered to hear their message—that colonial liberties must be upheld. The Sons of Liberty organized mass demonstrations to protest the Stamp Act, demonstrations that included setting fire to dummies resembling colonial officials. Such demonstrations often ended in chaos and rioting.

On April 26, 1766, less than six months after it went into effect, the Stamp Act was repealed. Americans had learned a valuable lesson from the experience: that Parliament could be forced to back down if the opposition was loud enough. The Sons of Liberty thought their work was done, and most groups disbanded. But Samuel Adams (1722–1803), a Boston Son, continued to keep the spirit of resistance alive in his city. Adams despised King George; he believed the king was plotting to destroy colonial liberty. His was one of the earliest voices to call for complete independence from Great Britain; most people had to be convinced over time that independence was necessary.

Samuel Adams spent much of the 1760s writing articles for Boston newspapers, reporting stories about British soldiers beating up on "innocent" citizens and attacking young women. Sometimes his stories were exaggerated, but many people accepted them as true. Adams is said to have provoked confrontations with British soldiers stationed in Boston, and he often staged mob violence from behind the scenes. Throughout the course of the American Revolution (1775–83), he took an active part in organizing resistance to Great Britain.

Townshend Acts

The Stamp Act was replaced with the Declaratory Act, which would prove to be just as bothersome. But America was so busy rejoicing over the repeal of the former that they paid little attention to the latter. The Declaratory Act stated that the British government had the power to make laws that would bind the colonists "in all cases whatsoever." Parliament then proceeded to test that right by making more tax laws to demonstrate its power over the colonies. The Declaratory Act of 1766 paved the way for the Townshend Acts of 1767, named for the King's adviser, Charles Townshend (1725–1767), who created them. The Townshend Acts called for taxes on lead, glass, paint, tea, and other items.

These taxes were the heaviest ever placed on the colonies, and they aroused intense criticism. According to historian William Lecky (1838–1903), from the time of the Townshend Acts onward, "the English government of America [was] little more than a series of deplorable blunders," meaning the king and Parliament made a lot of stupid mistakes in their handling of the colonies. Clearly, the British government was determined to raise money in the colonies by taxing them, no matter what the king's American subjects might say or do.

The Townshend Acts, named for King George's adviser Charles Townshend, called for taxes on lead, glass, paint, and other items. *(Reproduced by permission of The New York Public Library Picture Collection.)*

The Sons of Liberty revived in response to the passage of the Townshend Acts. Several important newspapers of the time were controlled by the Sons, and the news they published kept the public informed and the cause of liberty alive. The colonists reacted with renewed boycotts of British goods and escalating violence. Officials who tried to collect taxes were tarred and feathered (a painful and oftentimes crippling form of punishment in which a person is covered with hot tar and sprinkled with feathers).The tax collectors appealed to Governor Francis Bernard for protection, but he claimed he could do nothing. He told them that Bostonians would never let him get away with summoning British troops to patrol the city. Desperate, the tax collectors then appealed to the commander of the British Royal Navy stationed in Halifax, Nova Scotia (Canada). Commodore Samuel Hood was happy to help, and on his orders, a fifty-gun British warship sailed into Boston Harbor in the summer of 1768.

The Affair of the Letters

In 1773, the same year the Tea Act was passed (see Chapter 5: On the Brink of War [1770–1775]), an international scandal erupted over some letters that had been written by leading citizens of Massachusetts to influential people in England back in 1767–1768. Historians say the publication of these letters probably helped convince the British government that it was time to take drastic steps to put down the rebellion in the colonies. It was these steps that led to the American Revolution.

Key figures in the scandal were royal governor of Massachusetts Thomas Hutchinson (one of the alleged authors of the letters) and colonial agent Benjamin Franklin (one of the finders of the letters). Hutchinson, a Boston-born merchant turned colonial administrator, had a history of upholding all decisions made by the British government. Many critics agree that Hutchinson's policy of backing British authority no doubt hastened the move toward colonial revolution.

The letters that caused the uproar had been written after the passage of the Townshend Acts in 1767 and voiced an antipatriot sentiment. Americans were becoming increasingly irate over British attempts to tax them. Officials appointed to collect the taxes were abused and their property damaged or destroyed. Mobs rioted in the streets of Boston. The letters, said to be composed by Governor Hutchinson and others, described these and other events taking place in America. Once written, they were sent to key people in Great Britain.

Benjamin Franklin got hold of the letters while he was serving in London as a colonial agent for Massachusetts. Agents were representatives appointed by lawmaking bodies in the colonies to live in London, circulate among prominent people, and report back on what was happening in Parliament. The agents voiced the colonies' needs and wishes as Parliament prepared to make laws that affected colonial territory.

Franklin had watched as relations between England and America soured in the 1760s and early 1770s. He loved both countries and he could not understand why Parliament seemed so determined to upset and anger the colonists. One day in 1772, he thought he found the answer in

John Dickinson opposes Townshend Acts

Among the most eloquent objections to the Townshend Acts of 1767 were those voiced by American lawyer, politician, and author John Dickinson (1732–1808). The

a mysterious packet of letters given to him by a gentleman whose name he would not reveal. After reading the letters, Franklin came to believe that Parliament had taken harsh actions against the colonies at the urging of Governor Hutchinson and others like him.

Franklin felt that if the colonists knew about the bad advice coming from their own leaders, then colonial resentment toward Great Britain might cool and Parliament would have time to create and implement more appropriate policies. He decided to share his discovery with the Massachusetts legislature. Across the ocean and into the hands of Speaker of the Assembly Thomas Cushing went the packet of letters; they arrived in March of 1773. (The Massachusetts Assembly was the lower house of the legislature). Cushing was told to show the letters to whomever he wished, but not to publish them.

Samuel Adams got hold of the letters, though, and he did publish them. When American colonists read them—in particular the line "there must be a great restraint of natural liberty"—they were furious. Dummies representing Hutchinson were set on fire in Philadelphia and Princeton, New Jersey; poems were published comparing Hutchinson to evil rulers of ancient times; a popular play of the day accused him of selling "his native land." John Adams called Hutchinson a "vile serpent" and declared that his letters bore "the evident marks of madness." The letters convinced many Americans that the rumors spread by the Sons of Liberty were true—there were plots against their liberties brewing on both sides of the Atlantic Ocean.

The Massachusetts legislature petitioned King George III to remove Hutchinson from office. King George's advisers held a hearing and determined that the charges against Hutchinson were "false and erroneous" and "calculated only for the ... Purpose of keeping up a Spirit of Clamour [loud outcry] and Discontent" in the colonies. Shunned in America, Hutchinson sailed to England in 1774 and died there six years later. Franklin was called a thief for taking the letters in the first place, and he lost his well-paying job as deputy postmaster of the colonies. After this incident, Franklin's feelings toward Great Britain underwent a drastic revision.

Townshend Acts had received different reactions in the various American colonies. In the North, they were greeted with violence and fierce opposition. In the Middle and Southern colonies, there existed a large group of individuals who objected to the passage of the Townshend Acts but remained loyal to King George; this loyalty made them more inclined to go along with the acts. Dickinson tried to change their minds with his influential work, *Letters from a Farmer in Pennsylvania to Inhabitants of the British Colonies.*

The letters appeared in the form of essays addressed to "My Dear Countrymen." There were about a dozen in all, published first in newspapers and later in pamphlet form. Pamphlets—reading material with a paper cover—were a popular way of communicating at the time. In his letters, Dickinson pointed out that with the Townshend Acts, Parliament was trampling upon colonial rights. He claimed that Parliament had no right to tax the colonies but did have the right to regulate trade.

The letters were read widely in both England and America. Many Americans—and even some people in England—found themselves in agreement with Dickinson. His argument would turn up again and again in the many writings and speeches that appeared before the war for independence finally broke out.

Townshend Acts are repealed

The colonists continued to boycott British goods. Their efforts were successful, and British exports to the colonies fell off tremendously. Nervous British merchants saw their profits dwindling and pressured Parliament for a remedy. Finally, in 1770, all the Townshend taxes were done away with, except the one on tea.

The colonists were no happier with the tax on tea than they had been with the other taxes. As they fumed, the people of Boston were also growing annoyed with British soldiers, who had little to do but loaf around on the streets while being fed and housed at Bostonians' expense. Not surprisingly, tensions continued to mount.

For More Information
Books

Bushman, Richard L. "Revolution: Outbreak of the Conflict." In *The Reader's Companion to American History.* Edited by Eric Foner and John A. Garraty. Boston: Houghton Mifflin, 1991.

Fradin, Dennis B. *Samuel Adams: The Father of American Independence.* New York: Clarion Books, 1998.

Minks, Louise, and Benton Minks. *The Revolutionary War.* New York: Facts on File, 1992.

Sources
Books

Beard, Charles Austin. *The Beards' New Basic History of the United States.* Garden City, NY: Doubleday, 1960.

Canfield, Cass. *Sam Adams's Revolution (1765–1776).* New York: Harper & Row, 1976.

Catton, Bruce, and William B. Catton. *The Bold and Magnificent Dream: America's Founding Years, 1492–1815.* Garden City, NY: Doubleday, 1978.

Cook, Don. *The Long Fuse: How England Lost the American Colonies, 1760–1785.* New York: Atlantic Monthly Press, 1995.

Dolan, Edward F. *The American Revolution: How We Fought the War of Independence.* Brookfield, CT: Millbrook Press, 1995.

Johnson, Paul. *A History of the American People.* New York: HarperCollins, 1997.

Lecky, William E. Hartpole. *History of England in the Eighteenth Century.* 7 vols. New York: AMS Press, 1968.

Maier, Pauline. *From Resistance to Revolution: Colonial Radicals and the Development of American Opposition to Britain, 1765–1776.* New York: Alfred A. Knopf, 1972.

Marrin, Albert. *The War for Independence: The Story of the American Revolution.* New York: Atheneum, 1988.

Montross, Lynn. *The Reluctant Rebels.* New York: Harper & Brothers, 1950.

Morison, Samuel Eliot, and others. *The Growth of the American Republic.* Vol 1. New York: Oxford University Press, 1969.

Web Sites

"American Revolution Timeline: Prelude to Revolution, 1763–1775." The History Place. [Online] Available http://www.historyplace.com/unitedstates/revolution/rev-prel.htm (accessed on December 17, 1999).

On the Brink of War (1770–1774)

5

After Parliament's passage of the Stamp Act in 1765, violence in the American colonies escalated, especially in Boston, Massachusetts. Surprisingly, some of these disturbances were orchestrated by well-educated, upstanding, respectable adults who held a grudge against England. (It is interesting to note that just before the Revolutionary War started, about half the population of the colonies was quite young—under fifteen years of age. An entire generation of colonial youth, then, was raised in a culture of rebellion.)

People like Samuel Adams (1722–1803), who favored a break with England, used mob action to keep the spirit of independence stirring. Newspaper publishers objected to the Stamp Act requirement that decreased American profits on their papers, so they kept the people riled up, too—and not just by publishing fiery letters. It was the publisher of the *Boston Gazette* who provided the dummies dressed as stamp agents for burning by a mob gathered to protest the Stamp Act.

Large numbers of American colonists were convinced that the Boston Massacre was caused by out-of-control British soldiers. *(Reproduced by permission of The Library of Congress.)*

A massacre takes place in Boston

British soldiers had been sent to the Massachusetts colony in late September of 1768 to try and keep the peace, and their presence on the streets of Boston was a constant irritation to its citizens. "Soldiering was a low, nasty profession," noted Albert Marrin in *The War for Independence: The Story of the American Revolution.* The redcoats were an unsavory bunch of convicts, "dropouts, [and] no-goods.... Judges often gave prisoners a choice between the army or the noose."

Some soldiers harassed colonial women and children as they went about their daily business. On top of this, many colonists were—for a variety of reasons—having a hard time supporting themselves. Decent-paying jobs were in short supply, and because of a cutoff in trade with Great Britain, goods were scarce and higher prices were being charged for them. Yet, under the terms of the Quartering Act, the colonies were expected to provide food, housing, and supplies for British redcoat soldiers. The underpaid British soldiers often accepted odd jobs to supplement their incomes: they were viewed by unemployed colonists as unwelcome competition for work. It was only a matter of time before things got out of control.

On the afternoon of March 5, 1770, citizens and off-duty soldiers exchanged insults on the streets of Boston. Throughout the afternoon and early evening, mobs roamed the streets, taunting and provoking one another. Such incidents had occurred regularly throughout the nearly eighteen-month-long British military occupation of Boston. Finally, a series inflammatory remarks directed at a redcoat guarding the Customs House in Boston led to all-out violence. The soldier called for assistance, prompting British Captain Thomas Preston and several redcoat soldiers to race to his aid.

Verbal attacks gave way to a physical confrontation, in which colonists pelted the redcoats with stones, snowballs, chunks of ice, and clubs. After one of the redcoats was hit on the head, someone from the British side fired into the huge crowd of colonists that had gathered outside the building. Three people were killed outright; two were wounded and later died; six others were injured. According to one of the dying men, Samuel Adams had masterminded the bloody incident. But Adams claimed to be surprised and confused over the whole affair. It was probably Adams, though, who dubbed the incident the "Boston Massacre."

Differing views of the incident

Samuel Adams and his followers wasted no time in spreading the news far and wide: a "horrid Massacre" had taken place in Boston. Large numbers of American colonists were convinced that desperate Boston citizens had been forced to defend themselves against out-of-control British soldiers. (The troops were removed to a nearby island in the aftermath of the incident.) In fact, this version of the event was taught to generations of American schoolchildren. According to the British view, though, the soldiers had been driven to violence by the abusive and threatening actions of infuriated Boston citizens.

Captain Thomas Preston and eight of his men were arrested for the deaths that occurred that day in Boston. Preston offered a detailed account of the episode, beginning with "the arrival of his Majesty's troops in Boston [which] was extremely [hateful] to its inhabitants." He spoke of the "malicious temper of the people," an "alarming circumstance to the [soldiers]."

Captain Preston went on: "The insolence [insulting behavior] as well as utter hatred of the inhabitants to the troops increased daily." He then described the scene of utter chaos that occurred on the evening of March 5, with fire alarms ringing to call a colonial mob together. Finally, "one of the soldiers having received a severe blow with a stick, stepped a little on one side and instantly fired" without orders. A fight broke out, heavy clubs and snowballs were thrown, and "all our lives were in imminent danger." In the greater confusion, more shots were fired, several men fell, and the crowd ran away. "The whole of this melancholy [sad] affair was transacted [took place; occurred] in ... 20 minutes."

Boston Massacre followed by a brief calm

A trial was held, but little evidence was produced that Preston had ordered his men to fire. In all the confusion, it was difficult to even figure out who had done the shooting. Preston and six others were finally let go; two others were found guilty, branded (burned) on the hand, and released.

Paul Revere (1735–1818), a respected silversmith, engraved an image of "The Bloody Massacre" as he imagined it happened (engravings could be used to make many printed copies), and copies were circulated all along the East Coast. As Marrin pointed out, Revere seems to have altered the truth to increase sympathy for the colonists. His drawing depicts "Captain Preston, his sword raised ..., ordering the Redcoats to fire into the 'peaceful' crowd." The press continued to hammer home the point that liberty was being threatened. The publicity surrounding the episode contributed to growing anti-British feelings in the colonies.

Among cooler heads, however, there was a feeling that the violence had gotten out of hand. For a time, calm descended on the colonies, and matters returned to normal. Some trading resumed between England and the colonies (except for tea). England withdrew her troops from the western frontier (the troops were supposed to keep colonists out of Indian territory; see Chapter 4: The Roots of Rebellion [1763–1769]), and settlers began to move westward.

The mighty pen

While some people indulged in mob activities to show their distaste for British policies toward the colonies, others expressed their opinions through strongly worded writings. For ten years, from 1765 to 1775, Americans used their ideas about freedom and justice as forceful weapons in the struggle for their rights. With the exception of a few people like Samuel Adams, the majority of colonists were not pushing for independence during those ten years. Most colonists remained loyal to King George III (1738–1820; reigned 1760–1820). They did not wish to withdraw from the British Empire but only to reform it, to make it better. American patriots were engaged in a struggle to express their rights as English citizens under the British constitution.

The war of words began in 1764 with James Otis's (1725–1783) *Rights of the British Colonists Asserted.* (See Chapter 3: Literature and the Arts in the Revolutionary Era.) John Dickinson (1732–1808) followed in 1767–1768 with his *Letters from a Farmer in Pennsylvania.* Richard Bland offered *An Enquiry into the Rights of the British Colonies.* Samuel Adams contributed *A Statement of the Rights of the Colonies* in 1772. Two years later, Thomas Jefferson (1743–1826) offered his *Summary View of the Rights of British America,* which set out two of the themes that would run through the revolutionary struggle: the importance of individual rights and the notion of popular sovereignty (pronounced SOV-ruhn-tee)—meaning that the right to govern lies within a society and does not belong to kings.

Jefferson also scolded King George for having sent "amongst us large numbers of armed forces, not made up of the people here, nor raised by the authority of our laws." He appealed to the king to open his heart and mind to "liberal and expanded thought" and added, "Let not the name of George the third be a blot in the page of history.... Only aim to do your duty, and mankind will give you credit where you fail. [Don't continue] sacrificing the rights of one part of the empire to the ... desires of another: but deal out to all equal and impartial right."

In addition to individual writings, colonial legislatures bombarded the British government with petitions, in which they attempted to interpret their vision of American rights under the British constitution. Among those rights was the right to tax themselves.

The British government relented in 1770 and repealed all of the Townshend taxes (see Chapter 4: The Roots of Rebellion [1763–1769]), except the tax on tea (a very popular English beverage). Ironically, the repeal was passed on the very same day the Boston Massacre took place. It would be more than a month before Parliament heard about the violence in Boston and Americans heard that the tax on their tea had not been lifted.

King George is petitioned

In 1770 American statesman Benjamin Franklin (1706–1790) was serving as a colonial agent in England. He was living in London at the time, was well respected by the British, and had friends in Parliament. But even with his inside information, Franklin did not know that it was King George's idea to keep the tea tax in order to demonstrate British power over the Americans. When Americans found out that the tax on tea was to remain in effect, they concluded that King George must be getting bad advice from his ministers; otherwise, hearing their objections, he would have done away with the tax.

Colonial legislatures decided to change tactics, and they began to address their petitions directly to King George, thinking they would "educate" him about the evil actions of his advisers. Petition after petition was sent, with no reply from the king. His colonial subjects simply could not understand it. King George declared, "I shall always be ready ... to listen to the Complaints of my Subjects," but added that the tone of the petitions was "disrespectful to me, injurious to Parliament, and [not in accord with] the Principles of the [British] Constitution." In 1773 the *Massachusetts Spy* newspaper urged an end to the petitioning, calling it "degrading." Hopes of reasoning with King George began to dwindle in America. The mood in the colonies grew gloomier.

British views on the American colonies

As far as the British were concerned, Parliament had the absolute right to supervise the British Empire and to tax its subjects as necessary, without question. The Mother Country protected her colonies and needed tax money to pay for that protection. The colonies had to recognize that they were dependent members of the empire, not her equals—it had always been that way, and there was no reason to change.

British politicians and newspapers had much to say on the subject of American colonists who seemed to have forgotten that their purpose was to make profits for England. Surely they could not be so foolish as to think that taxes collected from Englishmen should be used for the benefit of Americans. John C. Miller quoted the opinions of the English in his book *Origins of the American Revolution:* "I have always regarded the Colonies as the great *farms* of the public, and the Colonists as our tenants," said one. Many looked upon "the American colonists as little more than a Set of Slaves, at work for us, in distant Plantations." Another Englishman gave voice to an opinion shared by most of his countrymen: "We sent them to those Colonies to labour for us.... For what purpose were they [allowed] to go to that country, unless the profit of their labour should return to their masters here?"

While a few English statesmen spoke for Americans as defenders of English liberties, King George had his own agenda, and an outspoken, disobedient America was not a part of it.

Lord North and British Parliament

In his first ten years on the throne, King George III went through five prime ministers. The prime minister was the head of Parliament, and Parliament had the power to make and carry out laws. If George wanted to have a hand in the lawmaking process, he needed a prime minister he could work with—one who would listen to his ideas and incorporate them into laws that would be passed by a majority of members of Parliament.

In 1770 King George at last found a man he liked in Prime Minister Sir Frederick North (1732–1792), better known as Lord North. North would hold the post for twelve event-filled years that spanned most of the American Revolution. Together, Lord North and King George continued stubbornly along the political path that resulted in England's loss of the American colonies.

For North's first two years in office, the atmosphere in the colonies was fairly calm. A peace-loving man, North was pleased. Parliament busied itself with other matters and was almost silent on the question of the American colonies. Then came the Tea Act of 1773.

The Tea Act was North's solution to a business problem. The British East India Company, a large trading business, was in danger of failing. Eighteen million pounds of East India Company tea was going to waste in a London warehouse, mainly because Americans refused to import (and pay taxes on) British tea. Under the Tea Act, small taxes would be charged on East India tea, but the company would be able to send the tea directly to American tea agents. Even with the tax, the tea sold by East India would be cheaper than any other tea sold by American merchants (smuggled in from other countries). It was North's hope that Americans would go along with the tax because the price of the tea would remain so low.

A tea party is held in Boston

The tea was to be delivered to a select group of agents who would reap big profits from its sale; other colonial merchants would be left out in the cold. Americans saw through Lord North's trick. The small tax on the tea was still a tax "without representation" in Parliament—and a clear example of the English flexing their political muscle over the colonies. Just as irritating was the threat the tax posed to American businesses.

Despite American objections, the tea was taken from the London warehouses and sent on its way to the colonies.

The citizens of Charleston, South Carolina, left the tea to rot in warehouses. In New York and Philadelphia, officials refused to allow the tea to be unloaded from trading ships. But Massachusetts Governor Thomas Hutchinson (1711–1780), a staunch defender of British authority (and the father of two of the men who were supposed to sell the tea), insisted that the tea-bearing ships in Boston Harbor remain there until the taxes were paid. In response, Samuel Adams and other Boston rebel leaders organized the Boston Tea Party.

On the night of December 16, 1773, a group of Boston patriots disguised themselves as Mohawk Indians. (The Mohawks were fierce warriors who painted their faces black before engaging in battle.) Armed with small hatchets and clubs, they went down to Griffin's Wharf, quietly boarded three ships at anchor there, and over the course of three hours dumped 342 chests of tea—more than 90,000 pounds' worth—into Boston Harbor. The day after the Tea Party, Founding Father John Adams (1735–1826) wrote in his diary: "This is the

The small tax on the tea was still a tax "without representation" in Parliament. In response, Samuel Adams and other Boston rebel leaders organized the Boston Tea Party.
(Reproduced by permission of the National Archives and Records Administration.)

A Participant Describes the Boston Tea Party

No one will ever know for sure who was actually present at the Boston Tea Party. Historians have spent years piecing together family stories and documents trying to determine who took part in it. Estimates of the number of participants range from 110 to more than 200.

Eyewitnesses claim the entire tea party was carried out in complete silence and that no one was hurt in the process. George R. T. Hewes, a thirty-one-year-old shoemaker, dictated his account of the event many years later. According to his version, the only violence came as a result of the tea-starved citizens of Boston trying to make off with their favorite beverage:

> During the time we were throwing the tea overboard, there were several attempts made by some of the citizens of Boston and its vicinity to carry off small quantities of it for their family use. ...[T]hey would watch their opportunity to snatch up a handful from the deck, where it became plentifully scattered, and put it into their pockets. One Captain O'Connor, whom I well knew, came on board for that purpose, and when he supposed he was not noticed, filled his pockets, and also the lining of his coat. But I had detected him and gave information to the captain of what he was doing. We were ordered to take him into custody, and just as he was stepping from the vessel, I seized him by the skirt of his coat, and in attempting to pull him back, I tore it off; but, springing forward, by a rapid effort he made his escape. He had, however, to run a gauntlet through the crowd [run through rows of armed guards] upon the wharf, each one, as he passed, giving him a kick or a stroke.

> Another attempt was made to save a little tea from the ruins of the cargo by a tall, aged man who wore a large cocked hat and white wig.... He had sleightly [cleverly; craftily] slipped a little into his pocket, but being detected, they seized him and, taking his hat and wig from his head, threw them, together with the tea, of which they had emptied his pockets, into the water. In consideration of his advanced age, he was permitted to escape, with now and then a slight kick.

Source: Hawkes, James, alleged author. A Retrospect of the Boston Tea-Party, with a Memoir of George R. T. Hewes, Survivor of the Little Band of Patriots Who Drowned the Tea in Boston Harbour in 1773. By a citizen of New-York.... New York: S. S. Bliss, printer, 1834. Quoted in The Spirit of Seventy-Six: The Story of the American Revolution as Told by Participants. Edited by Henry Steele Commager and Richard B. Morris. New York: Da Capo Press, 1995.

most magnificent Movement of all. There is a dignity, a Majesty ... in this last Effort of the Patriots that I greatly admire.... This Destruction of the Tea is so bold, so daring, so firm, intrepid and inflexible, and it must have so important Consequences and so lasting, that I cannot but Consider it as an Epocha [period of significance] in History."

Reactions to the Boston Tea Party

The Boston Tea Party marked a point of no return in relations between England and America. Clearly, defiance against England was in the air. But public opinion was divided over the dumping of the tea. Many people felt empowered and filled with pride after the tea party and were ready to forge ahead in the battle of wills with England. Others were troubled. Some Boston merchants, fearing a total disruption of business, offered to pay for the tea. Americans were forced to think hard about where they stood with respect to England's colonial policies.

Parliament was in no mood to make deals; the desire to punish the colonies was too strong. The British government considered the dumping of the tea to be a wicked and totally illegal action. British citizens were outraged, and public opinion was firmly set against America. Parliament regretted the 1766 repeal of the Stamp Act. Tired of the mob violence and disrespect in America, the Mother Country felt the need to show the colonies who was boss.

Lord North went before Parliament with several harsh proposals designed to punish the citizens of Boston. They included the Boston Port Act, the Massachusetts Government Act, the Administration of Justice Act, and an extension of the Quartering Act of 1765. Called by Parliament the Restraining Acts or the Coercive Acts, Americans referred to them as the Intolerable Acts of 1774.

The Intolerable Acts

Under the Boston Port Act, Boston Harbor would be closed to all trading and shipping activities until the East India Company was paid for the dumped tea. Even fishing boats could not enter the harbor. If this act remained in effect long enough, reasoned North, Boston's citizens would be starved into paying for the tea.

Under the Massachusetts Government Act, General Thomas Gage (1721–1787), chief of British forces in the colonies and newly appointed governor of Massachusetts (he replaced Governor Hutchinson), would assume complete control of town meetings. From the earliest days of colonial history, citizens had jealously protected their right to make deci-

What was King George Thinking?

It has been said that George III was not very bright—biographers claim that he was eleven years old before he learned to read. But he was a hard worker with a strong sense of duty, a man of simple tastes who enjoyed farming and country sports. Though he sometimes referred to the colonies as his "farms," the subject of America was of little interest to him.

By the time George III had ascended the throne in 1760 (he was twenty-two at the time), English kings no longer held the kind of absolute power they once did. The aristocracy—the upper-class minority—had taken over a large part of the king's authority and brought British Parliament under its control. Parliament passed all laws, and if King George wanted to have any legislative power, he had to befriend members of Parliament who would further his goals. Unfortunately, George clashed with many of the men he chose for the post of prime minister.

Then, in 1770, George appointed Lord North prime minister of Great Britain. Lord North faithfully carried out King George's orders and, in the process, helped drive the American colonists into revolt.

George viewed his role as ruler of the American colonies as that of a stern father dealing with a lot of unruly children. For the first ten years of his reign, he tried to keep his "children" in the colonies

sions for themselves at these meetings. To take away this right was, to them, an outrage. The Intolerable Acts would also place Massachusetts under military rule, meaning the colony would be controlled by the British army.

The Administration of Justice Act would protect British officials in the colonies. Those who were accused of committing major crimes while trying to carry out their duties would be tried in Great Britain, not the colonies. (Those duties included putting down riots and collecting taxes.)

In addition, the Quartering Act that had been passed in 1765 would be extended. The earlier act required colonists to provide housing and supplies to British troops in America for two years. In 1766 the act had been amended to permit the use of public buildings (such as inns) and unoccupied houses for British soldiers. On June 2, 1774, the act was extended to

contented; he even ordered his friends in Parliament to vote to repeal the Stamp Act.

But George grew impatient with anyone who disagreed with him on how to handle the swelling troubles in the American colonies. "I wish nothing but good," he asserted, "therefore everyone who does not agree with me is a traitor and a scoundrel." It was hard to argue with that kind of attitude. When news of the Boston Tea Party reached him, King George saw it as the first challenge to his personal rule, and he did not like it at all.

Up until the mid- to late 1760s, American colonists had few complaints about King George. They appreciated his youth and personality. But he clearly failed to respond to the needs and issues that were growing within the colonies. Americans began to feel that their liberties were being threatened by the British Empire. In response, the greatest minds in the colonies came together to voice the call for American rights.

Those who came forth to lead the colonies to freedom were some of the most remarkable individuals in history: John Adams, George Washington, Benjamin Franklin, Thomas Jefferson, Alexander Hamilton, James Madison, and countless others—people of sense, courage, education, far-sightedness, even genius.

include occupied buildings in all colonies; this could include private homes.

Reactions to Intolerable Acts

Parliament believed that once the colonies saw how Boston was being punished, all Americans would fall meekly into line. Lord North concluded his remarks to Parliament: "We must control them or submit to them." One by one, the acts were passed by Parliament, and by June of 1774, King George III had approved them all.

On June 1, the day the Boston Port Act went into effect, the citizens of Boston fasted and prayed. Church bells rang mournfully from morning until night, and public buildings were draped in black, the sign of mourning.

In response to King George's refusal to acknowledge the needs and issues of the colonists, the greatest minds in the colonies came together to voice the call for American rights. Thomas Jefferson was included in this elite group. *(Reproduced by permission of the National Portrait Gallery/Smithsonian Institution.)*

Parliament thought that Boston was the source of all its problems in the colonies, and everything would turn out all right if the Massachusetts town could be forced to submit. But since the Stamp Act had been passed, colonists in favor of a break with England had been hard at work throughout all the colonies, stirring up a spirit of rebellion and building a network of supporters. Samuel Adams sent word of the Intolerable Acts to his network (called Committees of Correspondence), and they rallied in support of Boston. Food, supplies, and messages of sympathy poured into the town from supporters throughout the colonies, and a new spirit of colonial unity arose from Boston's sufferings.

There were strong reactions against the acts throughout the colonies. From Baltimore came word that all her trade with the Mother Country would be suspended. In Philadelphia, angry mobs burned dummies representing tax collectors. Virginia's legislature called for a day of prayer in support of Boston.

Meanwhile, King George sent British redcoat soldiers to occupy Boston. Their job was to keep the city's unruly citizens in line and make sure the Intolerable Acts were enforced. The acts would be repealed in 1778, but by then it would be too late. The colonies were too deeply committed to independence to avoid a revolution.

For More Information
Books

Donoughue, Bernard. *British Politics and the American Revolution: The Path to War, 1773–1775*. New York: St. Martin's Press, 1964.

Franklin, Benjamin. *Poor Richard's Almanack, 1733-1758*. In *Benjamin Franklin Writings*. New York: The Library of America, 1987, pp. 1181–1304.

Johnson, Paul. *A History of the American People*. New York: HarperCollins, 1997, pp. 121–77.

Labaree, Benjamin W. *The Boston Tea Party*. New York: Oxford University Press, 1964.

Web Sites

Additional links can be accessed through "Yahooligans! Around the World: Countries: United States: History: Colonial Life (1585-1783): American Revolutionary War." [Online] Available http://www.yahooligans.com/Around_the_World/... (accessed on April 16, 1999).

Sources
Books

Adams, John. *John Adams: A Biography in His Own Words*. Edited by James Bishop Peabody. New York: Newsweek, 1973.

Commager, Henry Steele, and Richard B. Morris, eds. *The Spirit of Seventy-Six: The Story of the American Revolution as Told by Participants*. New York: Da Capo Press, 1995.

Dolan, Edward F. *The American Revolution: How We Fought the War of Independence*. Brookfield, CT: Millbrook Press, 1995.

Lloyd, Alan. *The King Who Lost America: A Portrait of the Life and Times of George III*. Garden City, NY: Doubleday, 1971, pp. 190–91.

Marrin, Albert. *The War for Independence: The Story of the American Revolution*. New York: Atheneum, 1988.

Miller, John C. *Origins of the American Revolution*. Stanford, CA: Stanford University Press, 1959.

Schouler, James. *Americans of 1776: Daily Life during the Revolutionary Period*. Williamstown, MA: Corner House, 1984.

Web Sites

"American Revolution Timeline: Prelude to Revolution, 1763–1775." The History Place. [Online] Available http://www.historyplace.com/unitedstates/revolution/rev-prel.htm (accessed on December 17, 1999).

"Boston Massacre" and "Boston Tea Party." *DISCovering U.S. History*. [Online] Available (password required) http://www.galenet.com (accessed on January 25, 1999).

"Captain Thomas Preston's Account of the Boston Massacre. (13 March 1770)." [Online] Available http://www.ukans.edu/carrie/docs/texts/preston.html (accessed on February 15, 1999).

Lexington, Concord, and the Organization of Colonial Resistance

6

By mid-1774 animosity (bitterness and hostility) between Great Britain and the American colonies had reached the boiling point. Poised on the brink of war with America, the British were wondering if the Americans would really fight. Most did not think so. England's Earl of Sandwich (1718–1792) declared: "These are raw, undisciplined, cowardly men." The colonies, it was thought, could never come together and fight as one. The British felt that the people of Virginia and the Carolinas would not fight Massachusetts's battles; they were "too wise to be caught in such a mouse-trap." One British soldier wrote to his father: "The rebels are the most absolute cowards on the face of the earth."

On the other hand, some British statesmen argued that the Americans were more than willing to fight for freedom—for those same liberties enjoyed by King George III's subjects back in England. British statesman and orator Edmund Burke (1729–1797) urged the repeal of the Intolerable Acts and the withdrawal of British troops from America. He told members of Britain's Parliament they were dealing with a people "who will die in defence of their rights." Lord Dartmouth (1731–1801; for whom Dartmouth College is named) tried to convince his colleagues that armies were not the best way to reason with Americans. Even Britain's prime minister, Lord North (1732–1792)—trusted adviser of King George and designer of the Intolerable Acts—looked hard for a peaceful way out of the crisis. Their plans and pleas were all rejected by a majority in Parliament.

Members of Parliament seemed not at all concerned with ideas about liberty but only with punishment. From America, British general and colonial governor Thomas Gage (1721–1787) warned Parliament: These people "are not the despicable Rabble too many have supposed them to be.... They are now Spirited Up by a Rage and Enthousiasm, as great as ever People were Possessed of."

The formation of the First Continental Congress

Patriot leaders (advocates of colonial authority) decided that the time was right for a formal meeting of representatives from all the colonies. Such a group could coordinate resistance to the British. As Virginia's lawmaking body, the House of Burgesses, stated: "We are ... clearly of opinion, that an attack, made on one of our sister colonies, to compel submission to arbitrary taxes [to force the colonies to pay unreasonable taxes], is an attack made on all British America, and threatens ruin to the rights of all, unless the united wisdom of the whole be applied."

An assembly known as the First Continental Congress met at Philadelphia's Carpenter's Hall in September of 1774 to discuss the colonies' next move. Fifty-six delegates—all of them men—from twelve colonies were chosen to attend (Georgia did not participate). They were men of strong beliefs and uncommon courage who knew well that their actions might be considered illegal by King George. For the most part, the delegates to the First Continental Congress were not wild revolutionaries, thirsting for confrontation. Many were lawyers, with a profound respect for the rule of law and the proper conduct of people in a civilized society. Some were wealthy merchants or planters; others, like Samuel Adams (1722–1803), were poor men.

Massachusetts was suffering the most from British oppression and needed the support of the other colonies in its ongoing struggle with the Mother Country. Well–known citizens James Bowdoin (1726–1790), Thomas Cushing, Robert Treat Paine (1731–1814), and John and Samuel Adams were chosen to represent the ailing colony. Thirty-eight-year-old John Adams (1735–1826) was the youngest of the delegates, and in his famous diary and in letters to his wife, Abigail, and others, he describes his journey to Philadelphia from Boston and his attendance at the Congress. His writings are considered the liveliest and most enjoyable version of what went on both in and out of Congress. Adams called the Congress "a nursery of American statesmen."

The group representing Virginia was quite distinguished and included Patrick Henry (1736–1799), Richard Henry Lee (1732–1794), Peyton Randolph (c. 1721–1775; who was elected president of the First Continental Congress), and George Washington (1732–1799). Patrick Henry had his first opportunity to show off his speaking skills before a large group of the best-educated and most influential men in the colonies. Colonists who favored a break with England were stirred by Henry's words, but those who were afraid to sever ties found it chilling when he boldly stated: "The distinctions between Virginians, Pennsylvanians, New Yorkers and New Englanders are no more. I am not a Virginian, but an American."

Pennsylvania sent Loyalist Joseph Galloway (c.1731–1803) to the First Continental Congress. (He opposed the idea of colonial independence and ended up moving to England when the revolution began. Pennsylvania charged him with treason [betraying his country] in 1788.) John Dickinson (1732–1808), whose writings earned him the title "penman of the Revolution," also represented Pennsylvania. (See Chapter 3: Literature and the Arts in the Revolutionary Era,

Fifty-six delegates—all of them men—from twelve colonies were chosen to attend the First Continental Congress (Georgia did not participate). They were men of strong beliefs and uncommon courage who knew well that their actions might be considered illegal by King George.
(Reproduced by permission of Corbis Corporation [Bellevue].)

This 1775 illustration titled "A Society of Patriotic Ladies at Edenton in North Carolina," shows patriotic women signing a proclamation that they will no longer drink tea. *(Reproduced by permission of The Metropolitan Museum of Art.)*

and Chapter 4: The Roots of Rebellion [1763–1769]).

From Connecticut came Roger Sherman (1721–1793), described by John Adams as "honest as an angel and as firm in the cause of American independence as Mount Atlas." New York sent John Jay (1745–1829), a wealthy judge from an old and distinguished family. He would represent the new nation as a diplomat to Spain and France. Delaware sent patriot Caesar Rodney (1728–1784), described by Adams as "the oddest-looking man in the world ... his face is not bigger than a large apple, yet there is sense and fire, spirit, wit and humor in his countenance." For this important gathering, the first of its kind, were gathered "fortunes, abilities, learning, eloquence [persuasive speakers], acuteness [sharp minds], equal to any I ever met with in my life," concluded Adams.

Getting down to business

It made sense that so many different kinds of people with different points of view would have varying opinions. Some delegates from the Southern colonies feared that those from Massachusetts wanted to take over the country. Other delegates thought that only the wealthy and well educated should have a say in decision-making for the colonies. Many delegates who were in business feared that defying England would ruin the established system of trade; instead of breaking ties with England, they wanted to find a way to restore good relations with the Mother Country.

Revolutionaries like Samuel Adams realized it was too soon to talk of independence, and they acted out of character by staying quiet for most of the First Continental Congress. John Adams recorded what went on at congressional meetings. Although he noted at one point that "it seemed as if we should never agree upon any thing," members were soon able to get down to business. In a surprisingly short time, several important documents were produced and approved.

Documents of the First Continental Congress

On October 14, 1774, Congress approved a Declaration and Resolves, which included a declaration of the rights of the colonies. This document, a model for the 1776 Declaration of Independence, stated in clear and dignified language that Parliament had no right to pass laws for the colonies. It listed every unlikable act passed by Parliament since 1763 and declared that "repeal of them is essentially necessary in order to restore harmony between Great Britain and the American colonies."

On October 20, 1774, Congress approved the Continental Association. The Association was important because it marked the first time that all the colonies agreed to join in a common goal—to penalize (punish or retaliate against) Great Britain in ways that would hurt her financially. The document stated the colonists' complaints and described plans for a boycott of British imports and exports that would remain in effect until their complaints were addressed. (A boycott is a refusal to conduct business with a certain source—in this case, Great Britain.) The colonies were one of Britain's major trading partners. One delegate predicted that the boycott measures adopted by the Association "must produce a national Bankruptcy [Great Britain would be ruined financially] in a very short Space of Time."

That same day, Congress prepared an appeal to King George III, outlining its complaints and rights and asking for his understanding. Americans still believed that King George was a fair man who was interested in the welfare of his subjects. The First Continental Congress adjourned on October 26, 1774, after agreeing to meet on May 10, 1775, if the king did not respond to the complaints in a satisfactory way.

King receives documents; Franklin pleas for peace

Even though King George probably read all the documents the Congress sent him, neither he nor Parliament gave

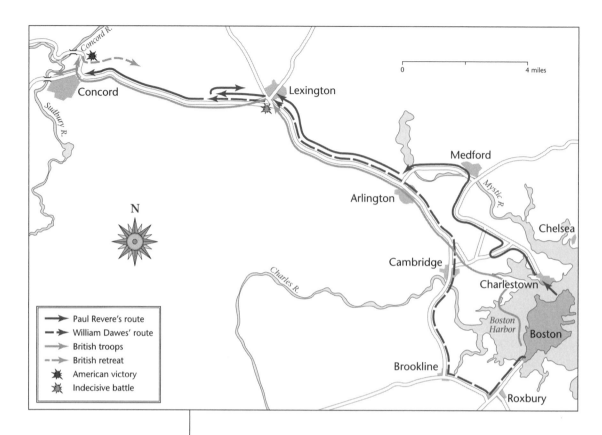

Map of the Battles of Lexington and Concord.
(XNR Productions. The Gale Group.)

any answer to the colonies. As far as George was concerned, the Continental Congress was an illegal body deserving no response. He did send a memo to his prime minister, Lord North, in which he said: "The New England governments are in a State of Rebellion. Blows must decide whether they are to be subject to this country or independent."

Benjamin Franklin (1706–1790) was in London while all of this was going on. A friend urged him to "contrive some means of preventing a terrible calamity and bring about a reconciliation." For three months, Franklin met both secretly and openly with America's friends in London, trying to avoid a war for independence.

In February 1775, as Franklin worked behind the scenes, he received word that Deborah, his wife of forty-four years, had died. Grief-stricken, Franklin left London for Philadelphia. By then he was disgusted with the "extreme corruption prevalent among all orders of men in this old rotten state" of England. He

was finally convinced that Great Britain was trying to keep itself alive by consuming the strength of the colonies.

Battles at Lexington and Concord: Two views

Since the passage of the Intolerable Acts in 1774, Boston had been awhirl in anger, protests, and rioting. Still, many patriots hoped war could be avoided. They were well aware that England was a formidable enemy (a major fighting force), while the widely scattered colonies had scant military experience. But, just in case the worst happened, the patriots decided to collect some weapons and store them in Concord, a small town about twenty miles northwest of Boston. Companies of minutemen were formed (men who could be ready to fight on a minute's notice), and committees of observation were appointed to watch and report on the activities of British troops.

Eight Americans were killed and one British soldier was wounded at the Battle of Lexington. Each side claimed the other fired first. Though undeclared, the American Revolution had begun. *(Reproduced by permission of Corbis Corporation [Bellevue].)*

On the night of April 18, 1775, Paul Revere rode from Boston to Lexington and Concord to prepare Americans for the arrival of British forces.

(Reproduced by permission of Archive Photos, Inc.)

In April 1775, British General Thomas Gage (1721–1787), then governor of Massachusetts, heard about the weapons buildup in Concord. He had been ordered by King George to take some definitive action and show Bostonians who was boss. Gage decided to send troops to Lexington and Concord to seize the weapons stashed there and to capture John Hancock (1737–1793) and Samuel Adams, two colonial freedom-fighters who were in hiding from British authorities. Massachusetts patriot-spies found out about Gage's plans almost instantly. On the night of April 18, Paul Revere (1735–1818) and William Dawes (1745–1799) rode from Boston to Lexington and Concord, respectively, to prepare Americans for the arrival of British forces. From their legendary rides came the famous line: "The redcoats are coming."

As British soldiers made their way across the Massachusetts countryside, church bells rang, warning drums beat, and guns were fired to alert citizens of their approach. At dawn on April 19, between 40 and 75 patriot soldiers gathered at

"The Call to Arms." As word of the approaching British forces spread, men across the colonies picked up their rifles and joined in the fight.
(Reproduced by permission of Archive Photos, Inc.)

Lexington to greet part of the British force of 700 men. Realizing they were outnumbered, the Americans were about to disband when the first shots were fired—shots that were "heard 'round the world." Eight Americans were killed and one British soldier was wounded. Each side claimed the other fired first. Though undeclared, the American Revolution had begun.

The British called for reinforcements. Before they arrived, 700 British soldiers marched on Concord, where they met resistance from a force of about 450 Americans. Again, guns fired, with each side denying responsibility for the first shot. The British began a retreat to Boston but met with even more resistance all along the way. When the smoke cleared, 49 Americans lay dead, and more than 40 were wounded or missing. On the British side, 73 were killed, 174 were wounded, and 28 were missing.

Immediately, propaganda artists set to work offering wildly differing versions of the events of April 19, 1775. (Propaganda is biased or distorted information spread by persons

More than 700 British soldiers marched on Concord, but the strength of only 450 patriots forced the British to retreat. *(Reproduced by permission of Archive Photos, Inc.)*

who wish to present only their point of view and thus further their own cause.) The *Massachusetts Spy* of May 3, 1775, presented this version of events:

> AMERICANS! *forever bear in mind the BATTLE OF LEXING-TON! where British Troops, unmolested and unprovoked, wantonly [maliciously] and in a most cruel manner fired upon and killed a number of our countrymen, then robbed them of their provisions, ransacked, plundered and burnt their houses! nor could the tears of defenceless women, some of whom were in the pains of childbirth, the cries of helpless babies, nor the prayers of old age, confined to beds of sickness, appease their thirst for blood!—or divert them from their DESIGN OF MURDER and ROBBERY!*

In England, it was reported that Americans had scalped British soldiers, both dead and dying. A British soldier's account of the Americans' treatment of his comrades appears in John C. Miller's *Origins of the American Revolution.* According to the soldier, the Americans were "full as bad as the Indians for scalping and cutting the dead Men's Ears and Noses off, and those they get alive, that are wounded and can't get off the

Ethan Allen Avenges Deaths at Lexington and Concord

Ethan Allen (1738–1789) was a very colorful character, a man used to speaking his mind in a forceful if sometimes inelegant way. According to Albert Marrin in *The War for Independence,* "He was said to be strong as an ox and brave as a lion. Settlers spent wintry nights telling about how he bit off the heads of nails and strangled bears with his bare hands."

In 1775 Allen was the commander of the Green Mountain Boys, a gang of young fighting men who were trying to prevent the New York colony from taking over their land in the "Green Mountain" area that later became Vermont. Allen and his "boys" sympathized with the struggle of the Massachusetts colonists against British policies.

By the spring of 1775, a Continental (colonial) army had not yet been formed and war had not been declared. Congress had authorized only defensive fighting, and Lexington and Concord fit that description. After the battles at Lexington and Concord, many Americans were ready for war—and they knew they were going to need weapons to fight that war. The Connecticut Committee of Safety approached Ethan Allen about taking Fort Ticonderoga on Lake Champlain in New York. The fort, which was held by the British, had a good supply of cannons and other assorted weapons. Allen was glad to be of help, for news of the battles at Lexington and Concord had "electrified [his] mind" and made him "fully determined ... to take part" in the American struggle.

Meanwhile, the Massachusetts Committee of Safety asked noted military leader Benedict Arnold for his assistance. On May 9, 1775, Allen, Arnold, and about 83 men crossed Lake Champlain under cover of darkness. At dawn, they surprised the fort's sleeping inhabitants, forty-five British officers and men who, according to Allen, were "old, wore out, and unserviceable." They took the fort without a single shot being fired. Allen told the fort's commander they did it "in the name of the great Jehovah [je-HOH-vah; God] and the Continental Congress."

Ground." The British army claimed to have burned only those houses from which patriot soldiers were firing and accused the Americans at Lexington of firing first. What's more, they complained, the Americans did not fight fairly, but "ran to the Woods like Devils," running from tree to tree, taking shots at the British, then falling to their bellies to reload, instead of remaining standing to present a fair target.

General Gage's report to the British secretary of war made the incident seem unimportant: "I have now nothing to trouble your lordship with, but of an affair that happened here on the 19th." When members of the British government heard the gory details that came later, they were stunned. Great Britain had never had to use force to control its American subjects. Clearly, the conditions were ripe for a war, and what was more, America had proved that her fighting men were not afraid to stand up to trained British soldiers.

The Second Continental Congress

When Benjamin Franklin arrived in Philadelphia on May 5, 1775, he was greeted with the news that British troops had marched on Lexington and Concord. A few days later, in retaliation, Ethan Allen and his Green Mountain Boys would seize Fort Ticonderoga, New York, a key fortification held by the British (see box titled "Ethan Allen Avenges Deaths at Lexington and Concord"). The news of the taking of Fort Ticonderoga would not be considered good by the Continental Congress. Members wondered how England would react to this act of aggression. Congress passed a resolution stating that the material seized at the fort should be held in storage until it could be returned—when harmony was restored between the colonies and Great Britain.

On May 6, Franklin was chosen to represent Pennsylvania at the Second Continental Congress. Thomas Jefferson (1743–1826) was appointed Virginia's representative. Jefferson would speak little at that meeting, but he would soon prove that his reputation of a "masterly Pen" (according to John Adams) was well deserved.

Since King George would not listen to their grievances, delegates forming the Second Continental Congress assembled in Philadelphia on May 10, 1775. This time they met in the more spacious State House. John Hancock of Massachusetts, then a fugitive from British justice for his resistance to British oppression, was elected president of the Congress. Within five weeks, Congress would face the agonizing reality that war with Great Britain was inevitable (could not be avoided).

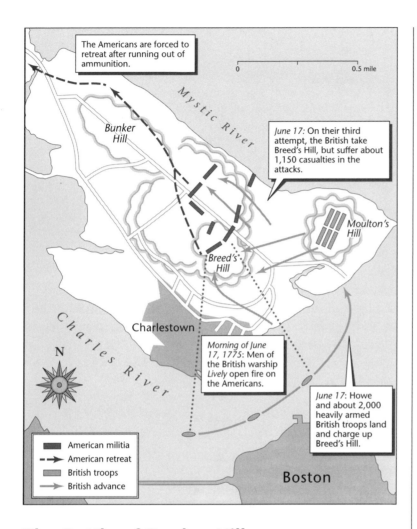

The Americans are forced to retreat after running out of ammunition.

June 17: On their third attempt, the British take Breed's Hill, but suffer about 1,150 casualties in the attacks.

Morning of June 17, 1775: Men of the British warship *Lively* open fire on the Americans.

June 17: Howe and about 2,000 heavily armed British troops land and charge up Breed's Hill.

Bunker Hill

Mystic River

Moulton's Hill

Breed's Hill

Charlestown

Charles River

N

Boston

American militia
American retreat
British troops
British advance

Map of the Battle of Bunker Hill. *(XNR Productions. The Gale Group.)*

The Battle of Bunker Hill

The seaport city of Boston lies at the mouth of the Charles and Mystic rivers. The Charles River separates Boston from the Charlestown peninsula, site of Breed's and Bunker hills. (A peninsula is a piece of land that juts out into the water.) South of Boston is another peninsula called Dorchester Heights.

In the early summer of 1775, the British controlled Boston. The two peninsulas around Boston were not yet claimed by either the British or the Americans, although American soldiers were lined up all around them. If the colonists could mount heavy guns atop the hills overlooking Boston on the Charlestown and Dorchester peninsulas, the British hold on Boston would be threatened. Britain's General Gage decided to take possession of the hills, but the Americans learned of his plan and devised one of their own.

As the British lay sleeping on the night of June 16, 1775, about 1,000 American militiamen under the command of Colonel William Prescott (1726–1795) joined General Israel Putnam (1718–1790) to dig trenches at the top of Breed's Hill; then, they sat down inside them. Spotting them the next morning, the men of the British warship *Lively* opened fire. The Americans, unaccustomed to the noise of battle, began to panic and run away. Colonel Prescott encouraged the men to stand firm. When, later that day, British General Howe and about 2,000 heavily armed men rowed across the Charles River to attack, General Putnam is said to have ordered the Americans to hold their fire until they saw "the whites of their eyes."

It was not the British fighting style to charge uphill, but they did it anyway. Clad in their red coats and carrying packs of equipment weighing nearly a hundred pounds each, they approached the American militiamen (who now numbered about 3,000) in disciplined waves—and became easy targets for the Americans at the top of Breed's Hill. The redcoats were repelled by colonial forces the first two times they tried to take the hill. On their third attempt, however, the British confronted the American rebels, who, by this time, were out of ammunition. After trying unsuccessfully to defend themselves with rocks, bayonets, and the butts of their muskets, American forces fled from Breed's Hill to nearby Bunker Hill. (Breed's Hill, then, was the true location of the battle, even though the ordeal is referred to as the Battle of Bunker Hill.)

When the smoke cleared, the British were in possession of both Breed's and Bunker hills. They could take little satisfaction in their "victory," however. About 1,150 highly trained soldiers were wounded or dead; the American force suffered 140 deaths and hundreds more injuries. The Americans—poorly trained, poorly equipped, and poorly organized—had put up a tremendous fight, retreating only when they finally ran out of ammunition. General Gage reported to his superiors in London: "The loss we have sustained is greater than we can bear." The British, who remembered the disorganized battles of Lexington and Concord and thought they were in for an easy time, were stunned to realize they were in for a hard fight. The siege (persistent attack) of Boston would last a full year.

Preparing for all-out war

At the end of June, word of the Battle of Bunker Hill finally reached Philadelphia. The Continental Congress found itself in a peculiar position. Many Americans were in a fighting mood, but war still had not been formally declared. A major question was, what kind of war—or peace—preparations should be made, if any? John Adams reported to a friend that the delegates in Philadelphia wanted to be prepared for any eventuality, so they planned "to hold the Sword in one Hand and the olive Branch [a symbol of peace] in the other." With these goals in mind, the Second Continental Congress—still hoping for reconciliation—petitioned for peace but simultaneously made preparations for war.

A majority of members of Congress supported John Dickinson, who wanted to continue the colonial appeal to King George. So yet another petition (the Olive Branch Petition) was prepared and sent to the king. John Adams called the whole procedure "silly." Although the petition was mild in tone, it was described in England as more "threats hissed out by Congress."

Like Adams, other members of Congress were convinced that reconciliation with Great Britain was no longer possible. Adams grew impatient, writing, "I was determined to take a Step, which should compel [congressmen] ... to declare themselves for or against something. I am determined ... to make a direct Motion that Congress shall adopt [an army] and appoint Colonel [George] Washington Commander of it." Adams's motion was made and passed.

Realizing that reconciliation with Britain was no longer possible, Congress decided to prepare for battle. George Washington took command of the Continental army on June 15, 1775.
(Reproduced by permission of Archive Photos, Inc.)

Why General Washington?

George Washington was a logical choice for the post of commander in chief of the American army. He had performed

Fighting Near Boston Shocks Americans

No formal declaration marked the opening of the Revolutionary War, but the bloody Battle of Bunker Hill (June 17, 1775) was an unmistakable sign that all-out war was just around the corner. The bloody incident was a tremendous shock to Americans. Soldiers and civilians alike were affected by the slaughter and its aftermath, as is made clear in the following excerpts. In the first, Colonel William Prescott describes the death of a soldier:

> *The ... man ... was killed by a cannon ball which struck his head. He was so near me that my clothes were besmeared with his blood and brains, which I wiped off, in some degree, with a handful of fresh earth. The sight was so shocking to many of the men that they left their posts and ran to view him. I ordered them back, but in vain. I then ordered him to be buried instantly.*

The rest of the quotations are taken from the writings of Abigail Adams, wife of Congressman John Adams. In her letters she describes the battle scene at Bunker Hill, complains that Congress is not doing enough to relieve the sufferings of the citizens of Boston, and comments on the condition of prisoners of war. John Adams was in Philadelphia with the Continental Congress when the battle took place. Abigail was left in charge of the family farm in Braintree, just south of Boston. From the top of Penn's Hill in Braintree, she could see the fighting going on at Bunker Hill. "The constant roar of the Cannon is so [distre]ssing that we cannot Eat, Drink, or Sleep," she wrote. She and her neighbors feared that the British army would soon be upon them unless Congress acted. "Does every Member [of Congress] feel for us?" she asked. "Can they realize what we suffer? And can they believe with what patience and fortitude we endure the conflict...?"

Bostonians were forbidden to leave their homes. Food was scarce, and British soldiers made life for the colonists virtually unbearable. In a letter to her husband, Adams describes the conditions endured by Americans taken prisoner at Bunker Hill:

> *Their living [conditions for Americans] cannot be good, as they can have no fresh provisions; their [the British] beef, we hear, is all gone, and their own wounded men die very fast, so that they have a report that the bullets were poisoned.... I would not have you be distressed about me. Danger, they say, makes people valiant. Hitherto [up until now] I have been distressed, but not dismayed. I have felt for my country and her sons, and have bled with them and for them.*

Sources: Richard Wheeler, Voices of 1776, *New York: Thomas Y. Crowell Company, 1972, p. 41. Lynne Withey,* Dearest Friend, *New York: The Free Press, 1981, pp. 60–68. Henry Steele Commager and Richard B. Morris, eds.,* The Spirit of Seventy-Six: The Story of the American Revolution as Told by Participants, *New York: Da Capo Press, 1995, pp. 150–51.*

brilliantly as a citizen-soldier on the British side in the French and Indian War (1754–1763; see Chapter 1: The People of the New World). Some historians speculate that if the British had promoted Washington at the end of that war, as he wished, he might have remained loyal to the Mother Country throughout the American Revolution. But he was not promoted, and when the British began placing heavy taxes on American colonists, Washington objected strongly.

Washington was a wealthy Virginia planter, and Virginia was the largest and wealthiest American colony—the one to which the other colonies looked for leadership. Washington was a commanding figure ("six foot two inches in his stockings and weighing 175 pounds"), and he was ready for another wartime adventure. The only member of the Second Continental Congress to attend sessions wearing a military uniform, Washington promised John Adams that if he were chosen to lead an army in battle: "[I'd] raise one thousand men, [feed and clothe] them at my own expense, and march myself at their head." John Adams noted: "There is something charming to me in the conduct of Washington. A gentleman of one of the first fortunes upon the continent, leaving his delicious retirement, his family and his friends, sacrificing his ease and hazarding all in the cause of his country!"

The nomination of Washington as commander in chief of a new Continental army was heartily approved by Congress on June 15, 1775. George Washington then made his way to Boston, and on July 3 he assumed command of the 17,000 soldiers in the American army.

"Our cause is just. Our union is perfect"

As Congress adopted measures to put the colonies in a state of readiness for war, it seemed a good idea to explain its actions to the world—to let the world know the justice of its cause. So on July 6, 1775 Congress adopted the Declaration of the Causes and Necessity of Taking Up Arms. It stated: "Our cause is just. Our union is perfect. Our internal resources are great, and, if necessary, foreign assistance is undoubtedly attainable." Congress declared that Americans were of "one mind resolved to die freemen rather than to live [as] slaves."

Before adjourning on August 2, 1775, the Second Continental Congress appointed commissioners to discuss the upcoming war with Native Americans and established a national postal system with Benjamin Franklin as its head.

On August 23, 1775, King George issued a Proclamation of Rebellion. In it, the king's men in the colonies were ordered to "exert their utmost endeavours to suppress such rebellion, and to bring the traitors to justice." On the same day Congress received this news, it received two other shocking pieces of information: 1) King George was planning to hire German soldiers to fight for him in a war against America, and 2) the British navy had, without cause, burned down the town of Falmouth, Massachusetts.

For More Information
Books

French, Allen. *The First Year of the American Revolution*. Boston: Houghton Mifflin, 1934.

Montross, Lynn. *The Reluctant Rebels: The Story of the Continental Congress, 1774–1789*. New York: Harper, 1950.

Ward, Christopher. *The War of the Revolution*. Edited by John R. Alden. New York: Macmillan, 1952.

Sources
Books

Adams, John. *John Adams: A Biography in His Own Words*. Edited by James Bishop Peabody. New York: Newsweek, 1973.

Alden, John R. *The American Revolution: 1775–1783*. New York: Harper & Row, 1954.

Dolan, Edward F. *The American Revolution: How We Fought the War of Independence*. Brookfield, CT: Millbrook Press, 1995.

Draper, Theodore. *A Struggle for Power: The American Revolution*. New York: Random House, 1996.

Marrin, Albert. *The War for Independence: The Story of the American Revolution*. New York: Atheneum, 1988.

Miller, John C. *Origins of the American Revolution*. Stanford, CA: Stanford University Press, 1959.

Web Sites

"American Revolution Timeline: Conflict and Revolution, 1775–1776." The History Place. [Online] Available http://www.historyplace.com/unitedstates/revolution/revwar-75.htm (accessed on January 20, 2000).

"American Revolution Timeline: Prelude to Revolution, 1763–1775." The History Place. [Online] Available http://www.historyplace.com/unitedstates/revolution/rev-prel.htm (accessed on December 17, 1999).

"Continental Congresses" and "The Battles of Lexington and Concord." *DISCovering U. S. History.* [Online] Available (password required) http://www.galenet.com (accessed on January 25, 2000).

Assembling an Army
(1775–1776)

7

Key political events occurring in the colonies in the summer of 1775 seemed contradictory. On the one hand, the Second Continental Congress was making a last attempt to avoid a break with Great Britain by sending the Olive Branch Petition to King George III (1738–1820; reigned 1760–1820). At the same time, however, George Washington (1732–1799) was appointed commander in chief of a new Continental army, and he was making preparations for war.

Washington took the responsibilities of his new post very seriously. He bought every military book the Philadelphia bookshops had on hand (about five) and read them from cover to cover. He also held meetings to discuss how to go about feeding and supplying a large group of men and their dependents. (This was not a simple matter in a time when everything had to be carried by horses, mules, or boats.) In addition, Washington assembled a network of spies (people who would watch the enemy secretly to obtain important information about their war plans) and gave them money from his own funds to start their work.

The generals who would serve under Washington were chosen by the Second Continental Congress. Washington took no part in the discussions in Congress, and he knew few of the men who were finally chosen as his generals. Delegates from each of the thirteen colonies fought to make sure their colony had its share of generals in the newly formed army. Founding father John Adams (1735–1826) was so annoyed over the petty fighting in Congress that he wrote: "Nothing has given me more torment than the scuffle we have had in appointing the general officers." When the debate was finally over, four major generals and nine brigadier generals had been named.

George Washington's generals

The most colorful of Washington's new generals was Charles Lee (1731–1782) of Virginia, known as a "soldier of fortune" because of his long history of serving in military campaigns both for profit and adventure. On one such campaign in the 1750s, he had been "adopted" by the Mohawk Indian tribe and had married the daughter of a Seneca Indian chief. The Seneca knew him as "Boiling Water" because of his fiery temper. Bold and forthright, Lee was unafraid to voice his opinions: he wrote to British leaders to inform them that they should make peace because America could not be conquered. This brave general's long experience as a soldier proved extremely valuable to Washington as plans for a Continental army were being implemented.

Artemas Ward (1727–1800) of Massachusetts was named major general (and second in command to General Washington). Ward was a stern, religious man who believed that the citizens of Massachusetts were God's chosen people. Ward and Washington did not get along. The friction between them probably began when Washington took over the command of Ward's soldiers in the Boston army (they formed the core of what would later be named the Continental army) and called them "the most indifferent people I ever saw ... exceedingly dirty and nasty people."

Another general, Philip Schuyler (pronounced SKY-ler; 1733–1804) of New York, was a well-educated man of Dutch descent. His powerful family had connections by marriage to most of the other important families in New York. He had served in the French and Indian War (1754–63; see Chapter 1: The People of the New World) and was a brilliant soldier, but many considered him too proud and condescending (meaning he acted superior to others). Washington, however, found his patience, good judgment, and attention to the details of managing an army to be of great value to the American cause.

Washington met his fourth major general, Israel ("Old Put") Putnam (1718–1790), for the first time in Cambridge (near Boston) on July 2, 1775. The fifty-seven-year-old farmer and tavern owner could barely read or write, but the fantastic stories surrounding his past had already made him an American folk hero. Although he stood only five feet six inches tall, legend had it that he had once killed a large wolf in her den and survived shipwreck and burning at the stake by Indians. Washington would discover that the aged hero, while eager to serve, was not highly respected by the young soldiers under his command and practiced a form of warfare that had become outdated.

On July 3, 1775, Generals Washington, Putnam, and Lee rode to the outskirts of Boston to inspect their troops.

New England militiamen are incorporated into Continental army

European nations fought their wars and defended themselves with professional soldiers, but things were different in America. The geography of the place—its sheer size—did not make the typical European military organization practical. The colonists needed some way to defend themselves against angry Native Americans. The Indians were not hostile toward them at first but became so after more and more colonists arrived in the New World and threatened to destroy the Natives' land, culture, and traditions.

The colonists protected themselves by forming a colonial militia (pronounced muh-LISH-uh). It consisted of every able-bodied man in the community. Each man understood that it was his duty to turn out and fight to protect his family and community in case of an attack. Men served for as long as they were needed—Indian attacks usually did not last long— then they returned home. The militia system proved to be the most practical defense for the colonies and was far less expen-

John Burgoyne arrived from England in the summer of 1775 to assist British General Thomas Gage. *(Source unknown.)*

sive than a professional army, especially since men brought their own weapons and supplies.

It was militia members from throughout New England who turned up at Lexington and Concord in April of 1775 and then forced the British to retreat to Boston. Somewhere between 16,000 and 17,000 militia men were encamped around Boston when George Washington assumed command in July. These men were ordinary citizens—many of them farmers or shopkeepers—and they were not used to fighting or handling weapons. They were loosely organized, without a high commander, and owed their loyalty only to the colony from which they came.

British warships were thick in Boston Harbor that summer, and three British generals—William Howe (1729–1814), Henry Clinton (1738–1795), and John Burgoyne (1722–1792)—had just arrived from England to assist General Thomas Gage (1721–1787). A group of soldiers accompanied them, bringing the total of British soldiers in Boston to 6,500.

Washington inspects his army

General Washington arrived in Boston nearly three weeks after the Battle of Bunker Hill to take command of what would henceforth be known as the Continental army. The British then held Boston, Charlestown, and the harbor. They could attack American forces by water, or they could head back to England at any time. The Americans occupied several spots—trenches or "earthenworks"—throughout a "Cemi Circle of Eight or Nine Miles" around Boston, according to a letter Washington sent to his brother.

When he gazed upon his troops, Washington could not believe his eyes. To the wealthy, upper class Virginian, the army

BOSTON

CHARLES TOWN

he was supposed to lead was an unencouraging sight. The volume *George Washington, Writings* contains a letter Washington wrote to his cousin and plantation manager, Lund Washington. General Washington described his regular soldiers as "an exceeding dirty & nasty people." He also reported that some of his officers were dishonest, "drawing more Pay & [supplies] than they had Men in their Companies."

Most of the soldiers did not even recognize Washington and therefore did not show him the kind of respect he deserved. Some had ideas of democracy that struck him as most peculiar, one being the notion that soldiers and officers were equals. The men Washington was supposed to command wandered from place to place, either ignoring efforts to discipline them or threatening those who tried. Washington wrote that the soldiers "regard[ed] their officers no more than broomsticks."

The fact that this was an army without uniforms contributed to the problem—it was hard to tell who was an officer.

Americans—poorly trained, poorly equipped, and poorly organized—had put up a tremendous fight at the Battle of Bunker Hill, retreating only when they finally ran out of ammunition. *(Reproduced by permission of the National Archives and Records Administration.)*

Washington threw all of his energy into making a disciplined army from this ragtag bunch. Officers were given colored armbands or knots of ribbons called cockades for their hats. Their men were put to work strengthening fortifications and camp sites that had been put together in a hurry and were already falling apart. Those who refused to work or recognize authority were punished. Those who tried to run away were caught, stripped, and lashed with a whip before being officially dismissed from the army. In *George Washington and the American Revolution* Burke Davis notes that, within a mere three weeks, Washington concluded: "We mend every day and I flatter myself that in a little Time, we shall work up these raw Materials into good Stuff."

Washington's men thought he was harsh (he had a violent temper that he never fully mastered) but fair. The patriotic public came by the thousands to have a look at him and were reassured by his self-confidence and distinguished good looks. But there were others who tried to destroy his reputation by printing falsehoods about him. In the colonies, people who remained loyal to King George attacked George Washington in newspapers, claiming he was disloyal. In London, *Gentleman's Magazine* printed letters describing a supposed love affair between the happily married—and very busy—Washington and "pretty little Kate, the washerwoman's daughter."

At this point in time, with war undeclared, Washington, his generals, and many Americans believed the struggle with Great Britain would last no longer than six months. Surely by then King George would read their petitions, and, knowing that America was ready to fight for its rights, he would be ready to make a deal. By summer's end, though, some colonists grew weary of America's "unofficial" war; they began to complain that Washington should stop wasting time training his troops and get busy attacking the enemy.

The fall of '75

While Washington continued with his war preparations, Congress continued to wait for a response from King George regarding its petitions for peace. In September 1775, Washington complained to Congress that he had no money to pay his men; he feared that after all his hard work, his soldiers would desert (abandon military duty) and there would be no army. Indeed, thousands had already gone home after the Battle of Bunker Hill. Congress sent a committee headed by Benjamin Franklin to discuss the situation. Steps were taken to provide money and supplies, and plans were made to build up an army of 20,000 men by calling on all the colonies for help. (Congress did not feel it had the authority to raise an army on its own.) The number of soldiers called ("quotas") depended on the population of the colony.

By mid-November, fewer than a thousand new men had enlisted. A month later, there were about 6,000 Continental ("regular") soldiers. Washington also had militiamen under his command, but he believed they were not reliable and could not be depended upon in battle. After their victory at Bunker Hill, the militiamen believed themselves to be outstanding soldiers; all they had to do was grab their guns and shoot at the British. They overlooked the reality that at Bunker Hill, they were behind fortifications, while the British fought out in the open. In short, they were more pleased with themselves than Washington thought they had any right to be.

Washington's new men were hunters, Indian fighters, and backwoodsmen from Virginia, Maryland, and Pennsylvania. They brought their own rifles and astounded everyone with their shooting skills. Their aim was so good they were put to work picking off British officers and soldiers who appeared in their line of fire. The British were outraged; they thought it was ungentlemanly for common soldiers to fire at officers. Despite their skills, though, the sharpshooters were a disorderly bunch, and, according to one source, Washington wished they had stayed at home.

During the early part of the war, the British stayed under cover for the most part, and Washington hesitated to attack. Throughout the fall, he had problems with his militiamen, who were hostile toward his "regular" soldiers. Everyone, including the British soldiers in Boston, soon grew bored and irritable with inactivity. Washington hoped that the British would attack him and force his hand, but they continued to sit in Boston and do nothing.

Keeping the army together

In October 1775, although still short of the 20,000 men he thought he needed, Washington issued an order that barred free black men from joining the Continental army (see Chapter 8: Blacks and Native Americans in the American Revolution). Free blacks had already proven their courage at the Battle of Bunker Hill; two African Americans—Caeser Brown and Cuff Hayes—are believed to have died there. But Washington was a planter and slaveholder from Virginia, and slave unrest was making Southerners nervous. Slaveholders feared that arming free blacks would be an invitation to disaster. Washington bowed to the pressure from the South and issued his order; a little over a month later, though, he was forced to reverse the order when the number of white soldiers willing to serve fell short of the number he needed.

By November, Washington's troops were healthy, well fed, housed, and trained to fight. But he had a problem. The soldiers' terms of duty expired at the end of the year. The enthusiasm they had felt after Lexington and Concord was beginning to wear off. Some of them began to leave early, taking their guns with them. After all his hard work, Washington faced the prospect of training an army all over again. He worried about what would happen if the British heard about this state of affairs. In a letter to his military secretary, Joseph Reed (who was on a leave of absence), Washington wrote: "Could I have foreseen what I have, and am likely to experience, no consideration upon earth should have induced me to accept this command." Washington had his generals try to coax the men into staying. One Connecticut soldier, Simeon Lyman, recorded in his journal how General Lee went about doing this:

> ...[W]e was ordered to form a hollow square, and General Lee came in and the first words was "Men, I do not know what to call you; [you] are the worst of all creatures," and flung and curst and swore at us, and said if we would not stay he would order us to go on Bunker Hill [then held by the British] and if we would not go he would order the riflemen to fire at us.

To Washington's relief, nearly half of the men due to leave reenlisted, and new troops began to trickle in from the South. In January 1776, Washington had 10,000 men under his command. Throughout the course of the war, though, he nearly always operated with far fewer men than he would have liked. Bonuses and bounties (rewards) were offered to entice recruits to sign on. And finally, because of manpower shortages and because victory seemed more important than the fears of slaveowners, the restrictions against black men serving in the army had to be reconsidered. By 1781, as the war drew to a close, it was estimated that as many as one-fourth of the Continental soldiers were black (see Chapter 8: Blacks and Native Americans in the American Revolution). But prejudice against blacks serving in the military was so strong that it would be another 200 years before the American army would again hold such a mix of black and white soldiers.

King George goes before Parliament

As Washington assembled his army around Boston, in London both the public and members of Parliament passionately debated British policies toward the colonies. The Bishop of Asaph warned Parliament and King George, "By enslaving your colonies you extinguish the fairest hopes of mankind." William Pitt the Elder, the Earl of Chatham (1708–1778), spoke before the House of Lords (the upper house of Parliament), declaring that "all attempts to impose servitude upon [Americans] ... will be vain, will be fatal."

In vain were all the warnings; on October 26, 1775, King George spoke before Parliament. He said, in part: "To be a subject of Great Britain ... is to be the freest member of any civil society in the known world.... The spirit of the British nation [is] too high," he added, "to give up so many colonies which she has planted with great industry, nursed with great tenderness, encouraged with many commercial [trade] advantages, and protected and defended at much expence of blood and treasure." Therefore, he said, he intended to put a "speedy end to these disorders" by enlarging his land and sea forces and by hiring foreign soldiers.

COMMON SENSE:
ADDRESSED TO THE
INHABITANTS
OF
AMERICA.
On the following interesting
SUBJECTS.

I. Of the Origin and Design of Government in general, with concise Remarks on the English Constitution.

II. Of Monarchy and Hereditary Succession.

III. Thoughts on the present State of American Affairs.

IV. Of the present Ability of America, with some miscellaneous Reflections.

Written by an ENGLISHMAN.
By Thomas Paine

Man knows no Master save creating HEAVEN,
Or those whom choice and common good ordain.
THOMSON.

PHILADELPHIA, Printed
And Sold by R. BELL, in Third-Street, 1776.

Common Sense, "by an Englishman," included a number of statements that would make the British consider its author, Thomas Paine, a traitor, including his reference to King George III as "the Royal brute of Great Britain." *(Reproduced by permission of Corbis-Bettman.)*

The debate in Parliament that followed this speech was long and spirited, but King George was unmoved. He set about raising an army, but his efforts were hampered by the fact that his cause was unpopular in England. His attempts to hire foreign soldiers were rejected in Russia and Holland, but the Germans obliged by selling the services of 30,000 soldiers. Most of them came from Hesse-Cassel (a region in southwestern Germany). Because of that, and because the three commanders in chief who led them through the war were from Hesse-Cassel, the men were called Hessians (pronounced HESH-uns). However, German mercenaries is a better description. Mercenaries (pronounced MER-suh-neh-reez; from the Latin word for "pay") are people who are hired for service in a foreign army.

The men from Hesse-Cassel, trained in the rigid European fighting style, were described by historian Burke Davis in *George Washington and the American Revolution* as "burly men with fierce mustaches and tarred queues [pronounced KYOOS; pigtails held in place with tar] who marched with the precision of marionettes." The Germans aroused both fear and anger among Americans, who could not believe that King George would hire soldiers to fight against his own subjects.

Common Sense convinces wavering Americans

In late 1775, with battles already fought at Lexington and Concord and at Bunker Hill, many Americans were still unwilling to make a final break with Great Britain. Many historians credit their change of heart to the publication of a pamphlet called *Common Sense*. Its author, Thomas Paine (1737–1809), was a self-taught champion of the common man who arrived in America from his native England in 1775 (see Chapter 3: Literature and the Arts in the Revolutionary Era). On January 10, 1776, Paine published his fifty-page pamphlet anonymously (without his name). *Common Sense*, "by an Englishman," included a number of statements that would make the British consider Paine a traitor, including his reference to King George III as "the Royal brute of Great Britain."

Paine wrote *Common Sense* in an easy-to-understand style. He emphasized the evil King George had done, citing instances of British misdeeds that were both true and fictitious (made-up). He wrote of murders of innocent women and children and of the burning of entire towns by the British—true incidents that had occurred at Falmouth, Massachusetts—in October 1775, and at Norfolk, Virginia, on January 1, 1776. Paine declared in *Common Sense* that 1) England was overtaxing Americans, 2) the English form of government with the king at its head was corrupt, 3) there was little sense in an island thousands of miles away governing the American continent, and 4) any colonist who was not prepared to fight had "the heart of a coward." On the topic of American independence, Paine wrote: "The sun never shined on a cause of greater worth."

Paine's pamphlet became America's first "bestseller"; according to the author's estimates, 120,000 copies were sold in three months. George Washington himself said it turned the tide in favor of independence, and he had it read to his troops. Washington noted: "I find *Common Sense* is working a powerful change in the minds of men."

The siege of Boston

In the aftermath of the Battle of Bunker Hill in June 1775, more than half of Boston's citizens had fled the city. Thousands of bored British soldiers remained stationed there while fourteen hundred of their comrades lay in the hospital, recovering from wounds or the epidemics of smallpox and fever that swept through the region. Fuel was scarce, and so was food. Morale sank very low as each side waited for the other to make a move.

The only advantages to the situation were that Washington had time to train his army, and volunteer (later General) Henry Knox (1750–1806) had time to sneak away and perform a virtual miracle. At his own expense, and with considerable difficulty, Knox recovered and brought to Washington the cannons (they were pulled by oxen) won by Ethan Allen (1738–1789) at Fort Ticonderoga, New York (see Chapter 6: Lexington, Concord, and the Organization of Colonial Resistance).

The war of nerves finally ended when Washington attacked first. On March 2, 1776, his troops began to fire on Boston. British soldiers could not believe their eyes when they beheld the huge cannons Washington had pointed at them. The attack went on for five days until suddenly, on March 8,

An Innocent Englishman Trapped in Revolutionary America

Nicholas Cresswell (1750–1804) was the son of an English sheep farmer and landowner. The young man was employed helping his father on his country estate when, at age twenty-four, he made the fateful decision to see America. The year was 1774, and the American Revolution was brewing. It was hardly an ideal time to be traveling to the colonies. Cresswell kept a diary of his visit, which was later published under the title *The Journal of Nicholas Cresswell: 1774–1777*. It offers a lively account of his adventures as America prepared for and engaged in a major war.

Cresswell traveled throughout the South, observing the customs of the people and engaging in trade with the Native Americans he encountered. (He traded money for animal skins.) He complained that his travels were often disrupted by war preparations. Cresswell found himself in a terrible position in late 1775 after all exports to Great Britain were stopped. No ships were sailing in either direction, and he had run out of money. Here are excerpts from his diary reporting on his distress:

"*Alexandria, Virginia—Thursday, October 19th, 1775.* Everything is in confusion, all exports are stopped and hardly a possibility of getting home. I have nothing to support me and how to proceed I do not know.

"*Friday, October 20th, 1775.* Slept very little last night owing to my agitation of mind. To add to my distress, the Moths have eaten two suits of my clothes to pieces.

Howe sent word to Washington that he was abandoning the city. Howe told Washington that if the Americans held their fire, he and his British troops would leave Boston undamaged.

Delayed by bad weather, it was not until March 17 that more than thirteen thousand British soldiers, sailors, women, children, and Loyalists (people loyal to Great Britain) set sail for Canada. Washington then assumed control of the suffering city of Boston, which had been rid of the British presence once and for all. (He later received a gold medal from Congress for what was considered a great victory at Boston. Congress wrote to congratulate Washington for his outstanding achievement in turning "an undisciplined band of husbandmen [farmers]" into soldiers.)

Nothing but War talked of, raising men and making every military preparation.... This ... is open rebellion and I am convinced if Great Britain does not send more men here and subdue them [the colonists] soon they will declare Independence.

"*Saturday, October 21st, 1775.* I am now in a disagreeable situation [because] if I enter into any sort of business I must be obliged to enter into the service of these rascals and fight against my Friends and Country if called upon. On the other hand, I am not permitted to depart the Continent and have nothing if I am fortunate enough to escape the jail. I will live as cheap as I can and hope for better times.

"*Monday, October 30th, 1775.* The people here are ripe for a revolt, nothing but curses ... against England, her Fleets, armies, and friends. The King is publicly cursed and rebellion rears her horrid head.

"*Tuesday, October 31st, 1775.* Understand I am suspected of being what they call a Tory (that is a Friend to my Country) and am threatened with Tar and Feathers, Imprisonment and the [Devil] knows what. Curse the Scoundrels."

In July of 1777, Cresswell finally made his way to New York and a ship bound for England. He left convinced that the once-happy land of America had been totally ruined by the stubbornness of "a vile Congress" and the blindness of King George.

Source: Nicholas Cresswell. The Journal of Nicholas Cresswell: 1774–1777. London: Jonathan Cape, 1918, pp. 126–28.

Back in London, the abandonment of Boston was seen as a great disgrace to the British Empire. Now, having failed in their mission to crush the rebellion in Massachusetts, the British came up with another strategy. The new plan was to rest in Canada, await troops and supplies being sent from England, then move south to conquer major Loyalist centers. One such center was New York City. Whoever controlled New York's Hudson River would have a tremendous military advantage. Rivers were major transportation routes for soldiers and supplies.

Charleston, South Carolina, was another major Loyalist center. Author Paul Johnson estimated in *A History of the American People* that "fully half the nation," if they did not call themselves Loyalists, at least "declined to take an active part" in the Revolution. Using major American cities as bases, the British expected to isolate New Englanders—the most troublesome of Americans—from the rest of the colonies and, hopefully, crush the rebellion.

George Washington already suspected that the British were planning to take New York. News of the proposed attack, combined with the stirring sentiment of *Common Sense* and Washington's success at Boston, convinced members of Congress that a drastic step had to be taken.

Composition of the fighting forces

Historians like to discuss how the mighty British military organization was defeated by a motley bunch of rebel soldiers. The British relied on professional soldiers. According to historians Allan Millett and Peter Maslowski, George Washington himself had fought alongside those soldiers in the French and Indian War, and he had the highest respect for them. Washington distrusted militiamen; he thought they were not respectful and too likely to panic and desert when the going got rough. He often had to rely on them, though, because short-term service in the militia was much more appealing to American men than long-term duty in a poorly equipped army.

Leadership roles in the British military went to officers, usually from the upper classes (often the younger sons of members of the nobility). These younger sons could never inherit the family money (it went to the oldest son), so they usually pursued careers in either the military or the church. Washington tried to mold his army into one just like the British model—officers, he said, should be "Gentlemen, and Men of Character"—but he was frequently disappointed in his officers. They were often sick, ignored his orders, or deserted. In the spectacular case of Benedict Arnold (1741–1801), Washington endured the hurt of having a trusted officer betray the cause by going over to the British side.

The lower ranks of the British military came from England's lowest social class. They were men who had nowhere else to turn and joined for the money or because the king forced them into service. The lower ranks of the American military consisted of some farmers and merchants, as well as recent immigrants, enemy deserters, prisoners of war, Loyalists, criminals (who were given the choice of enlisting or hanging), the homeless, servants, free black men, and runaway slaves. There was such a mix, in fact, that to some soldiers, the Indians they encountered near their homes seemed more familiar than their fellow soldiers.

Many of the Americans who fought for freedom believed in their cause and willingly endured tremendous hardships in defense of it. Millett and Maslowski summed it up: "Money could not buy, and discipline could not instill, the Continentals' type of loyalty; a ... motivation that promised a better life for themselves and their posterity [future generations] held them in the ranks." Despite George Washington's constant frustration with his men, he did manage to win the war with them.

Fighting styles—American versus British

One of the great questions debated by historians is how Washington pulled it off—how America won the Revolutionary War. Great Britain was one of the world's foremost military powers. Her navy was the world's finest. Her soldiers and seamen were well trained, well armed, and disciplined. American soldiers lacked experience, training, adequate weapons, and often even clothing and shoes. In fact, the colonies had no navy at all at the beginning of the war.

The American fighting style clearly gave the colonists the edge in their fight for independence. White men learned this rougher style by observing Native Americans as they fought to prevent whites from taking over their hunting grounds. The only reason the whites emerged the victors in their conflicts with the Indians was because they were better armed. Historian Arthur M. Schlesinger described what white soldiers learned from warfare with Indians in his book *The Birth of a Nation:* "In Indian fashion they now also scoured the woods, moving swiftly in small bands unimpeded with heavy baggage, sleeping in the open, living off the land, and stealing through the underbrush to spring surprise attacks."

Americans ignored rigid European-style rules of warfare. Like the Indians, American fighting men took full advantage of the cover provided by rocks and trees. Since Indians preferred not to fight in the winter, Americans often chose that season to attack. The unwillingness to fight in the wintertime was a European custom that would prove fatal to the British and their German allies in the Revolutionary War. American soldiers sometimes resorted to outright trickery, too, as when patriot militiamen were able to penetrate the British ranks at the Battle of Bennington, Vermont (August 1777) by fashioning rosettes—ornaments designed to resemble roses—into a style that was supposed to identify them as Loyalists.

In contrast, the British fought in the traditional European style. In Europe, wars were typically fought by opposing armies who drew close together on open, level terrain. According to military historian T. Harry Williams, because of the type of weapons they used, "men who wanted to kill other men in the eighteenth century had to be able to see their intended victims." Men marched onto a battlefield in columns, then formed lines of infantry (men with handguns) standing shoulder to shoulder, together with their artillery (men who operated weapons such as cannons that throw projectiles [bombs] across the field of battle). The cavalry (men on horseback) were stationed in the rear.

European battles began with artillery fire from both sides. Then, whichever commander thought he had the upper hand ordered his infantrymen forward. The men advanced in rigid lines, approaching within a hundred yards or less of the enemy. They halted and waited for the command to fire. After firing, the first line of men moved to the rear to reload or knelt so their comrades could fire over them. Albert Marrin noted in *The War for Independence:* "The idea was for many men to point their guns in the same direction, fire at once, reload quickly, and fire again in the hope of hitting something." This went on until the enemy infantry was thought to have reached the breaking point; then the winning commander would try for a rush with the cavalry.

As described by Harry T. Williams in *The History of American Wars from 1745 to 1918,* the cavalry came forward, shooting short guns at close range before drawing their swords and sweeping through the enemy ranks. When the field was won, the victors pursued the fleeing enemy. The defeated commander tried to elude the victors and regroup for another battle.

The British style of fighting required highly disciplined soldiers who had gone through long and rigorous training. This description in no way applied to the Americans, whom the British called "Yankees." (The term "Yankee" referred to any inhabitant of New England; when the British used the expression, they did not mean it as a compliment.) British soldiers had a very low opinion of the Yankees as fighting men, believing they would run for cover at the first sign of danger.

General Thomas Gage, commander in chief of British forces at the time of the Battle of Bunker Hill, remarked that the Yankees "will be Lyons, whilst we are Lambs but if we take the resolute part [if we are determined] they will undoubtedly prove very meek [mild; weak]." He was proven wrong, as the American soldiers held onto the hill until they ran out of ammunition (see Chapter 6: Lexington, Concord, and the Organization of Colonial Resistance).

The weapons they carried

British infantrymen carried handguns called flintlocks that were six feet long, including the bayonet (a knife that fit in the muzzle [shooting] end). T. Harry Williams described the loading of a flintlock:

> It was loaded from the muzzle, the man doing the loading having to stand in an exposed position. He bit off the end of an envelope containing ball and powder, rammed home the charge, placed priming powder in the pan, and was ready to fire. On command, he pressed the trigger, whereupon, if everything went right, a piece of flint struck steel, producing sparks that ignited the powder. The process required seventeen motions, but a trained soldier could get off two to three rounds a minute if he did not become rattled in the din of battle.

> The projectile discharged was a large lead ball that killed, or tore a gaping, ghastly wound, if it hit an enemy. It did not always hit, however.... Its most effective range was 50 to 100 yards. The Revolutionary officer [Colonel Putnam at the Battle of Bunker Hill] who reportedly [ordered] his men, 'Don't fire until you see the whites of their eyes,' was not making a statement for the history books but giving a necessary order.

Some American militiamen were equipped with a type of handgun that had been invented in the colonies. Known either as the Pennsylvania or Kentucky rifle, it had an accurate range of up to 300 yards. It took a long time to load, though, and

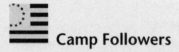

Camp Followers

Eighteenth-century armies bore little resemblance to today's armies. Men, women, and children known as "camp followers" played an important role in the American Revolution. They accompanied American soldiers as they traveled throughout the country during wartime. (British and German soldiers had camp followers during the war, too.)

Camp followers were not from any particular social class. Among them were: soldiers' wives or lady friends; educated women who were able to write letters for the soldiers, knit warm clothes and blankets, and manage battlefield hospitals; civilian (non-soldier) drivers of wagons; storekeepers who carried items for the soldiers to purchase; and clergymen.

Camp followers lived hard lives; they were expected to earn their own way and follow camp rules or suffer punishment. Those who obeyed the rules received a portion of food and drink. The followers had to keep up with the marching soldiers and often carried the unit's pots and pans along with the soldiers' personal belongings. Sometimes, pregnant women and the wives of officers were permitted to travel in military wagons. The women washed and mended clothing, made meals, and nursed the wounded. Commanding officers expected them to register their names and those of their children, along with that of the soldier to whom they were attached.

Women and children usually stayed in the military camps while the men went off to fight. But when battles became fierce, women such as Margaret Corbin (1751–c. 1800) and Mary McCauley (known as "Molly Pitcher"; 1754–1832), who were called half-soldiers, took off for the battlefront to assist their mates.

But camp followers could also be a danger to the army. For example, some American camp followers once wandered off to plunder houses that the enemy had abandoned. They brought back smallpox germs in the blankets they stole from the houses, and some soldiers were infected.

could be impractical in battle. More soldiers carried muskets, a type of shoulder gun. American-made artillery was in short supply, and Congress had to set up foundries (places where metals are cast [melted and molded]) to produce it. Stimulated by wartime needs, factories for the production of muskets and artillery sprang up throughout Massachusetts and Pennsylvania. What Americans could not manufacture was later imported from France—including more muskets and gunpowder.

Throughout the war, the British maintained the superiority in weaponry. Richard L. Bushman summed up the unexpected victory of the Americans this way: "[I]n the final analysis it was the refusal of the civilian population to [give up] and the determination of hundreds of ill-trained, poorly supplied companies to harass the enemy that weighed most heavily in the defeat of the British forces in America."

Congress orders formation of a navy

At the same time it was trying to put together a Continental army, Congress tried to establish a navy to go up against the world's greatest sea power—that of Great Britain. This was a much harder task than trying to form an army. While most potential army soldiers showed up to serve bearing their own weapons, a navy required expensive ships, complicated weaponry, and men trained to use them.

John Paul Jones was promoted to captain of the Continental navy in 1776, and in 1787 was the only Continental navy officer to receive a gold medal from Congress for his daring war exploits. *(Reproduced by permission of Archive Photos, Inc.)*

Efforts to create a navy were hampered throughout the war by a lack of shipbuilding facilities, so the Continental navy never grew to be very large. According to T. Harry Williams, only fifty to sixty ships ever served in the war—and not all at the same time. The highest number ever assembled to serve at one time was twenty-seven in 1776. In contrast, the British Royal Navy had 270 ships at the beginning of the war and 480 at the end of it (in 1783). Still, the Continental Congress hoped that a small American navy might at least slow the British down by creating a nuisance and disrupting British supply ships.

Congress never appointed a commander in chief of the Continental navy. Williams suggested one reason: among the few men who might qualify for such a position, there was too much jealousy to allow one of them to command the others.

Instead, each American ship acted independently, raiding British ships for supplies and weapons and sometimes engaging them in battle.

The most famous of the American sea raiders was John Paul Jones (1747–1792). Born in Scotland, John Paul added the "Jones" when he moved to America in 1773 or 1774 to conceal some unsavory actions in his past. According to Mark M. Boatner III's *Encyclopedia of the American Revolution,* Jones once beat a man for neglect of duty. The man died; Jones was charged with murder, and imprisoned, but the charge was later dismissed. On another occasion, a man ran into Jones's sword and died. Although it was not his fault, Jones's reputation suffered and his friends advised him to move to America.

He had been trained by the British Royal Navy and was the most knowledgeable of all American seamen when, in 1775, he was made a senior first lieutenant (pronounced loo-TEN-ant) in the new Continental navy. He was only twenty-eight years old. Jones was promoted to captain within a year and in 1787 was the only Continental navy officer to receive a gold medal from Congress for his daring war exploits.

The bravery of Jones and other raiders made America proud, but their actions were no match for the British Royal Navy. Throughout the war, the Royal Navy landed troops all along the American coast with little real interference. Henry Steele Commager summarized the naval campaign: "The story of the sea battles and naval campaigns of the American Revolution is a nautical version of [the biblical story of] David and Goliath [an ancient tale of an underdog going up against a giant]. The British Navy enjoyed overwhelming superiority over the tiny Continental naval force...." The balance shifted only once, when France and Spain entered the war on the side of America and French ships briefly controlled American waters (see Chapter 11: The War Shifts to the South [1778–1780]).

For More Information
Books

Hawke, David. *The Colonial Experience.* Indianapolis: Bobbs-Merrill, 1966.

Miller, Lillian B. *"The Dye Is Now Cast": The Road to American Independence, 1774–1776.* Washington, DC: Smithsonian Institution Press, 1975.

Sources

Books

Boatner, Mark M. III. "Knox's Noble Train of Artillery." *Encyclopedia of the American Revolution.* Mechanicsburg, PA: Stackpole Books, 1994, pp. 587–88.

Bushman, Richard L. "Revolution." In *The Reader's Companion to American History.* Eric Foner and John A. Garraty, eds. Boston: Houghton Mifflin, 1991.

Commager, Henry Steele, and Richard B. Morris, eds. *The Spirit of Seventy-Six: The Story of the American Revolution as Told by Participants.* New York: Da Capo Press, 1995.

Cresswell, Nicholas. *The Journal of Nicholas Cresswell: 1774–1777.* London: Jonathan Cape, 1918, pp. 126–28.

Davis, Burke. *George Washington and the American Revolution.* New York: Random House, 1975.

Johnson, Paul. *A History of the American People.* New York: HarperCollins, 1997.

Lyman, Simeon. "Journal of Simeon Lyman of Sharon, Aug. 10 to Dec. 18, 1775." In *Connecticut Historical Society Collections,* VII (1899), pp. 111–33.

Millet, Allan R., and Peter Maslowski. *For the Common Defense: A Military History of the United States of America.* New York: The Free Press, 1984.

Schlesinger, Arthur M. *The Birth of a Nation.* New York: Alfred A. Knopf, 1968.

Washington, George. *George Washington, Writings.* Edited by John Rhodehamel. New York: Literary Classics of the United States, 1997.

Williams, T. Harry. *The History of American Wars from 1745 to 1918.* New York: Alfred A. Knopf, 1981.

Native Americans and Blacks in the American Revolution

8

Native Americans and blacks fought on both sides during the American Revolution. Native American participation began in the earliest days of the conflict when, in March of 1775, the Massachusetts Provincial Congress accepted an offer from the Stockbridge Indians to form a company of "minutemen" (armed soldiers who promised to be ready in a minute to defend the colonies against the British).

In the face of war, the Continental Congress wrestled hard with the trying issue of Anglo-Indian relations. Congress was well aware that a close relationship existed between Great Britain and some Native groups, especially the powerful Six Nations Iroquois Confederacy (an association of six tribes: the Mohawk, Oneida, Onondaga, Cayuga, Seneca, and Tuscarora. The first five of the tribes originated in present-day New York. The Tuscarora came from North Carolina.) Congress also knew that Native Americans had many grievances against the colonists: white settlers had threatened their people and stolen their land. If large numbers of Indians chose to side with the British, such an alliance could easily contribute to America's defeat.

Realizing they were not likely to secure cooperation from most Native Americans in a war, Congress hoped to at least gain a promise of neutrality (noninvolvement) from them (see Chapter 4: The Roots of Rebellion [1763–1769]). On August 25, 1775, four commissioners appointed by Congress met with the Six Nations Iroquois Confederacy near Albany, New York, and delivered a speech, stating, in part: "Brothers and friends!... This is a family quarrel between us [the white colonists] and Old England. You Indians are not concerned in it. We don't wish you to take up the hatchet against the king's troops. We desire you to remain at home, and not join on either side, but keep the hatchet buried deep."

The Six Nations agreed to pledge neutrality. In the fall of 1775, the Western Nations (the Shawnee, Wyandot, and others) also agreed to remain neutral.

Other tribes took advantage of wartime to express their hostility toward Americans. The Cherokee, for example, staged an uprising in 1776 against settlers in Georgia and the Carolinas, but they were soon put down by American soldiers. Seven years later, the Cherokee lost much of their land in the treaty that ended the Revolutionary War.

Even some of the nations in the Iroquois Confederacy ended up taking sides in the war—despite their earlier pledges of neutrality. Most supported the British, although some favored the Americans. During the terrible winter at Valley Forge, Pennsylvania (1777–78), for example, the Oneida people brought corn to George Washington's troops, boosting their spirits and helping to ensure their survival (see Chapter 10: The Agonizing Path to Victory [1777–1778]).

Heavy participation by Indians on the British side began back in 1776, when the British under General John Burgoyne (1722–1792) were chasing the Americans out of Canada. Burgoyne urged the Six Nations to "take up the hatchet" against the Americans; he is said to have accompanied the urging with gifts and alcohol.

Burgoyne anticipated problems with his Indian recruits and tried to head them off with a famous speech he made on June 23, 1777. In his speech (quoted in Mark M. Boatner III's *Encyclopedia of the American Revolution*) he urged the Indians to fight "humanely." "I positively forbid bloodshed,

when you are not opposed in arms," he declared. "Aged men, women, children and prisoners must be held sacred from the knife or hatchet, even in the time of actual conflict.... [Y]ou shall be allowed to take the scalps of the dead when killed by your fire and in fair opposition; but on no account ... are they to be taken [otherwise]." (Note that North American Indian warriors often cut part of the scalp and hair from a defeated enemy as a souvenir of victory. This ancient custom was also seen as a way to capture a dead person's spirit, making it impossible for the victim to haunt his or her killer.)

Most of the Indians listening to Burgoyne's speech probably couldn't understand his English. The entire address was considered quite amusing in America and Great Britain— especially laughable was the thought that the Indians would change their fighting style to suit the British. (Many of Burgoyne's Indians deserted when he tried to make them fight his way.) But the laughter turned to outrage when news broke of the murder of Jane McCrea.

Many innocent men, women, and children were slaughtered during the Cherry Valley Massacre. American forces retaliated by burning Indian villages. In the painting above, Jane Wells pleads for her life as a Mohawk Indian prepares to kill her.
(Reproduced by permission of The Library of Congress.)

White Views of Native Americans

As uninformed and stereotypical as it sounds to us today, it was common for eighteenth–century Americans to refer to Indians as "savages." Not all colonial Americans held Indians in such low regard, however. Founding Father John Adams, like many other colonists, grew up near Native American families in Massachusetts and considered them good neighbors. Benjamin Franklin admired the Indians and had high praise for the Iroquois Confederacy, whose form of government was the inspiration for the democratic (government by the people) ideals in the Articles of Confederation (1781) and its successor, the Constitution of the United States (1789). In his 1783 essay "Remarks Concerning the Savages of North-America," Franklin wrote: "Savages we call them, because their manners differ from ours, which we think the Perfection of Civility; they think the same of theirs."

The Jane McCrea tragedy

McCrea was a young American woman who was engaged to one of General Burgoyne's soldiers. While on her way to meet her fiancé at Fort Edward, New York, in July 1777, she was apparently taken by a band of Burgoyne's Indians. Two days later, McCrea's scalped and bullet-ridden body was found near Fort Edward. Exactly what happened to the young woman remains a mystery. A tremendous uproar followed, and the tragic story of Jane McCrea grew into a legend.

Americans were horrified by the thought of a combined British-Indian invasion; inflamed by the tragedy of Jane McCrea, many rushed to join the fight against Burgoyne.

Violence escalates

The American Revolution had a profound effect on the longstanding harmony that had characterized the Iroquois Confederacy. Pro-British Iroquois tribes proved to be the greatest Native menace to the American cause when they participated with Loyalists (Americans loyal to Great Britain) in a series of raids on frontier communities in 1778–79. The most famous of the raids were the Wyoming Valley (Pennsylvania) Massacre of July 3–4, 1778 and the Cherry Valley (New York) Massacre of November 11, 1778.

For the Indians, as for Americans, the conflict had become a civil war. Brother fought against brother, and many brave warriors lost their lives. One of the survivors was Mohawk chief Joseph Brant (1742–1807; Indian name Thayendanegea, meaning "bundle of sticks"), a staunch supporter of the British. He had established a reputation for himself as a brilliant soldier and spokesperson for his people. Brant led his warriors in lightning-fast raids on frontier rebel targets. His very name filled the patriots with terror. Although he acted with white Loyalists, Brant took most of the blame for the horrid Cherry Valley Massacre, in which many innocent men, women, and children were slaughtered. American forces retaliated by burning Indian villages.

The postwar fate of Native Americans

In the 1783 Treaty of Paris that ended the American Revolution, the British gave up to the Americans all Indian lands as far west as the Mississippi River. This left pro-British Indians at the mercy of Americans, who were not inclined to be generous. It was generally believed that by helping the British, the Indian tribes gave up their rights to land within the United States. The new nation felt it was justified in forcing the Indians to retire to Canada or to the unknown areas beyond the Mississippi.

Joseph Brant, his Mohawks, and some other Indians relocated to Canada, where they continue to live today. Over the years, the Indians who remained in America were forced to give up most of their land. Even the two Iroquois nations who had fought with the Americans—the Oneida and the Tuscarora—were persuaded to sell their lands and move west as more and more whites intruded on their territory.

Mohawk chief Joseph Brant took most of the blame for the horrid Cherry Valley Massacre, in which many innocent men, women, and children were slaughtered. *(Reproduced by permission of the National Archives and Records Administration.)*

America's black soldiers

Between 8,000 and 10,000 blacks served in the Continental army at one time or another, comprising about a quarter of America's armed forces (see Chapter 7: Assembling an Army [1775–1776]). When the army was finally disbanded in 1783, about 5,000 so-called free blacks were told they could return

A black soldier named Salem wounded British Major Pitcairn during the Battle of Lexington.
(Reproduced by permission of Corbis Corporation [Bellevue].)

home. In reality, some of the 5,000 were slaves, but the need for soldiers had been so critical that no questions were asked when slaves claimed to be free men and sought to join the military.

After Congress set quotas—the number of soldiers each state was required to provide—some slaves were bought and freed by states that could not meet their quotas; they were then sent to serve with white soldiers in the Continental army. Massachusetts, Connecticut, and Rhode Island met their quotas by buying and freeing slaves and forming all-black units.

The Rhode Island Regiment, consisting of ninety-five slaves and thirty free blacks, distinguished itself at the Battle of Rhode Island in August 1778. When Count de Rochambeau, a French general, arrived in Rhode Island in 1780 to begin training French and American troops, one of his aides remarked that the Rhode Island Regiment was "the most neatly dressed, the best under arms, and the most precise in its maneuvers" of all the American soldiers.

Crispus Attucks Dies in the Boston Massacre

Crispus Attucks (c. 1723–1770) has been called the first black American to die for his country. Attucks, who was thought to be of African, Native American, and white ancestry, was probably born on an Indian reservation near Framingham, Massachusetts. The details of his youth are uncertain, but he is believed to have been a Christian, may have once been a slave, and was known to have worked on the Boston docks. The story of his death in the Boston Massacre (see Chapter 5: On the Brink of War [1770–1774]) has become a legend.

According to *Black Defenders of America* author Robert Ewell Greene, eyewitness accounts of events on the night of March 5, 1770 place Attucks at the head of a mob of "wrathful townsfolk" ready to attack British soldiers. "[C]rying out, 'Let us drive out these ribalds [pronounced RIB-uldz; crude, offensive, unprincipled persons; rascals]. They have no business here,' Attucks and his followers proceeded to assault British soldiers" with snowballs, rocks, and pieces of ice; some sources say that he and about thirty of his sailor friends were armed with heavy clubs.

Attucks and his comrades continued taunting the redcoats. Finally, a riot broke out, and Attucks began assaulting British soldiers with either a club or a gun he had seized in the scuffle. Voices in the crowd cried to the redcoats, "Why don't you fire?" Hearing this, a soldier who had been knocked to the ground opened fire as he arose. Attucks was killed by bullets to the chest.

Newspapers of the day used the incident to illustrate how the British were threatening American liberties, but few people in the colonies defended the rioting. The Sons of Liberty claimed no responsibility for planning it; some Sons, in fact, had urged the crowd to go home. The question remains: Were Attucks and his fallen companions heroes slaughtered in the quest for justice or rioters killed in mob violence?

Virginia slaves in the Revolution

Southern states, fearing slave uprisings, resisted the enlistment of black soldiers until late in the war. Virginia, the colony with the largest number of slaves in its population, would not allow slaves to carry weapons. Instead, in 1780 Virginia voted to meet its quota by offering rewards to any white man who enlisted for the duration of the war. The reward would be 300 acres of land and the choice of either a healthy

Crispus Attucks has been called the first black American to die for his country. *(Reproduced by permission of The Library of Congress.)*

black male slave between the ages of ten and thirty, or money.

Some Virginia slaveowners sent slaves to serve in the army in their place, promising them their freedom as a reward. Hundreds of these black soldiers returned to Virginia after the war, expecting to be freed. Upon their return, though, many were forced back into slavery. This was so obviously unjust that in 1783, Virginia's lawmaking body passed a bill aimed at slaveowners who, "contrary to principles of justice and to their own solemn promise," kept those black former soldiers as slaves.

Slavery weighs against the colonies

From the beginning of the Revolutionary War, black slaves took advantage of the wartime confusion to escape from their owners by the thousands. Many ran to the British.

An English court's 1772 decision in a lawsuit brought by an American slave probably swayed many slaves to support the British in the American Revolution. The case involved James Somersett, a black slave who was taken from Virginia to England by his owner, Charles Steuart. Somersett ran away, was captured, and was sent in chains on a ship bound for Jamaica (an island in the West Indies where slaves worked on sugar plantations). On board the ship, Somersett sued for his freedom. In June 1772, English Lord Chief Justice William Mansfield (1705–1793) issued his decision in the Somersett case, stating that slavery "is so odious [hateful], that nothing can be suffered to support it." He declared that because English law did not allow or approve of slavery, "the black [and any other slave who set foot in England] must be discharged [set free]".

In September, when news of Judge Mansfield's decision reached the colonies and the ears of black slaves, a period of unrest followed. This was especially true in Virginia, where 250,000 slaves were concentrated (the total population of the colonies was about 1.5 million; about one-third of colonial people were slaves). The Mansfield decision outlawed slavery in England, not in the colonies, but this did not matter to American slaves. Thinking that King George was on their side, many slaves ran away, hoping to get to England—and freedom. Their owners lived in constant fear of a slave revolt.

In 1775, with Revolutionary War battles already fought, Dunmore, the British-appointed governor of Virginia, added to slaveowners' fears by proclaiming that he intended to free rebel-owned slaves who would take up arms against their white owners. By December of that year, about 300 runaway slaves had joined Lord Dunmore's Ethiopian Regiment, as the military unit was called. (Ethiopian is an outdated term for black Africans.) Within six months, at least 800 more slaves had joined up with Dunmore. Outraged Virginia lawmakers responded by ordering the death penalty to "all Negro or other Slaves, conspiring to rebel" against their owners.

William Howe (1729–1814), the general in charge of British forces in America, finally put an end to the use of slaves in King George's army. It is impossible to know how many free blacks and slaves joined the British side, but certainly many more would have served if the British had allowed them to. For in a country where talk of freedom was widespread, many blacks were enslaved and would continue to be long after the American Revolution ended in 1783.

Runaway Southern slaves, many of them children, also served in the German military units hired by King George III. Hundreds served the British and Germans as laborers, servants,

A Trusted Spy

French soldiers had worked with blacks for years because the French controlled land in Africa. The Marquis de Lafayette (1757–1834), a close associate of General George Washington during the American Revolution, enlisted a black Virginian to act as a spy for him. The man was called James Armistead because he was the "property" of a slaveowner named William Armistead. His reports about enemy activities proved so useful, and he won such high praise from Lafayette, that the Virginia legislature eventually granted James his freedom. Lafayette returned to America in 1824 and looked up his old comrade. By that time James was calling himself James Lafayette.

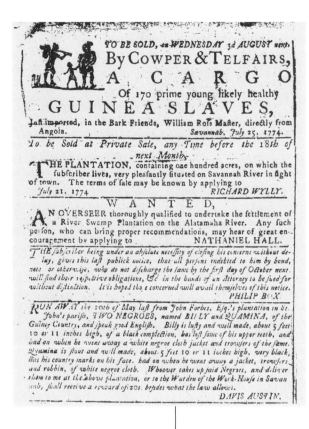

TO BE SOLD, on WEDNESDAY 3d AUGUST next,

By Cowper & Telfairs,

A   C A R G O

Of 170 prime young likely healthy
GUINEA SLAVES,
Just imported, in the Bark Friends, William Ross Master, directly from
Angola.   Savannah, July 25, 1774.

To be Sold at Private Sale, any Time before the 18th of
next Month,

THE PLANTATION, containing one hundred acres, on which the
subscriber lives, very pleasantly situated on Savannah River in sight
of town. The terms of sale may be known by applying to
July 21, 1774   RICHARD WYLLY.

W A N T E D,

AN OVERSEER thoroughly qualified to undertake the settlement of
a River Swamp Plantation on the Alatamaha River. Any such
person, who can bring proper recommendations, may hear of great en-
couragement by applying to   NATHANIEL HALL.

Hundreds of slaves fled to the British side to fight, in return for their freedom. Advertisements like the one above continued to draw business, and the slavetraders continued to prosper. *(Reproduced by permission of The Library of Congress.)*

drummers, fifers (flute players), and even as soldiers. When the war was over, some former American slaves—along with their wives and children—went to Germany with their employers. Some of the French took advantage of the confusion at war's end to re-enslave many blacks and sell them in the West Indies.

Blacks in the postwar years

After the American Revolution ended in 1783, pro-British former slaves could not stay in America. The new United States was still a slaveowning country. Runaway black slaves who had fought for the British became the targets of hatred by white Americans. They could not go to the West Indies because the economy of those islands depended on slave labor; there was no room there for large numbers of free blacks who might stir up the slaves. Nor could they go to London and other major cities in Britain because of the severe economic problems plaguing these areas in the postwar period.

The British felt that the problem could be solved by sending the former slaves to Nova Scotia, the easternmost part of the Canadian wilderness owned by Great Britain. An unknown number of pro-British blacks, together with thousands of British ex-soldiers looking for a new life, descended on the sparsely populated land in the mid-1780s. They were not welcomed warmly by Nova Scotians. Finally, in 1790, a former slave by the name of Thomas Peters sailed to London with a petition signed by several hundred black families. The petition sought assistance from the British government for the blacks living in Nova Scotia. In response, arrangements were made for them to sail from Nova Scotia to the western coast of Africa, where sympathetic English citizens were establishing a safe haven for Britain's poor free blacks.

Austin Dabney, Black Soldier in the American Revolution

Austin Dabney was a mulatto (pronounced muh-LAH-toe; a person of mixed white and black [then called Negro] racial heritage) and a slave. Slave status was transferred through mothers to their children. Since his mother was black, it did not matter if Dabney's father were free; it was his fate to be a slave. Dabney was sent to serve in the Revolutionary War in the place of his white owner. (This was a common and legal practice of the day, however unfair it may seem to us today.) He served bravely in the war against the British until the day he was wounded and given up for dead on the battlefield.

On February 4, 1779, while fighting the battle of Kettle Creek, Georgia, Dabney received a crippling musket shot to the thigh. He would have died there if he had not been found and rescued by a white American farmer named Giles Harris. Harris took Dabney to his home and nursed him back to health. In return, Austin Dabney—at this point a free black man—devoted the rest of his life to the Harris family, working for Harris and his children on the farm and even saving up his money to help finance a law school education for Harris's eldest son. Dabney later received a land grant for his service in the war. He and the Harrises are believed to have farmed that land together for several years before moving to Georgia's Pike County in 1826. Dabney died in Zebulon, Georgia.

Sources: Robert Ewell Greene, Black Defenders of America, 1775–1973. Chicago: Johnson Publishing Company, 1974, pp. 8–9. From George R. Gilmer, Sketches of the First Settlers of Upper Georgia. Baltimore: Baltimore Genealogical Publishing Co., 1965. Courtesy of Georgia Department of Archives and History, Atlanta, GA. Also see Scott, Carole E. "Georgia's Black Revolutionary Patriots." [Online] Available http://www.westga.edu/~cscott/dabney.html (accessed on January 19, 2000).

On January 15, 1792, a fleet of British ships set sail from Nova Scotia's Halifax harbor carrying several thousand people of African descent to the newly founded western African coastal settlement. This settlement, then known as Liberia (meaning "freedom"), is now the nation of Sierra Leone; its capital city is called Freetown. For more than half a century after the first blacks arrived there, many more black Americans would give up hope of obtaining freedom and equality at home and, like thousands before them, set sail for West Africa.

For More Information

Books

Nardo, Don, and Martin Luther King, Jr. *Braving the New World: 1619–1784: From the Arrival of the Enslaved Africans to the End of the American Revolution.* Milestones in Black American History Series. New York: Chelsea House, 1995.

Periodicals

"Black Soldiers Fought for Freedom during the Revolution." *Philadelphia Tribune,* February 9, 1999.

Web Sites

"History of the Black U.S. Soldier." [Online] Available http://www.cyberessays.com/History/143.htm (accessed on August 2, 1999).

Sources

Books

Boatner, Mark M. III. "McCrea Atrocity," "Burgoyne's Proclamation," and "Indians in the Colonial Wars and in the Revolution." *Encyclopedia of the American Revolution.* Mechanicsburg, PA: Stackpole Books, 1994.

Franklin, Benjamin. *Benjamin Franklin: Writings.* New York: Library of America, 1987.

Greene, Robert Ewell. *Black Defenders of America.* Chicago: Johnson Publishing, 1974.

Johnson, Paul. *A History of the American People.* New York: HarperCollins, 1997.

Lyons, Oren R., and John C. Mohawk, eds. *Exiled in the Land of the Free: Democracy, Indian Nations, and the U.S. Constitution.* Santa Fe, NM: Clear Light Publishers, 1992, pp. 102–4, 196, 246, 253, 257–64.

Marrin, Albert. *The War for Independence: The Story of the American Revolution.* New York: Atheneum, 1988.

Ploski, Harry A., and James Williams, eds. "Blacks in Colonial and Revolutionary America" and "Black Servicemen and the Military Establishment." In *Reference Library of Black America,* Vol. 3. Detroit: Gale, 1990, pp. 795–830.

Trevelyan, George Otto. *The American Revolution.* Edited by Richard B. Morris. New York: David McKay Co., 1964.

Washburn, Wilcomb E. "The American Revolution and Its Aftermath." In *The Indian in America.* New York: Harper & Row, 1975.

Williams, T. Harry. *The History of American Wars from 1745 to 1918.* New York: Alfred A. Knopf, 1981, pp. 3–82.

Web Sites

Selig, Robert A. "Black Soldiers of the Revolution." [Online] Available http://americanrevolution.org/blk.html (accessed on July 14, 1999).

A Ragtag Force Enters the Revolution (1776–1777)

9

 New York was one of the Middle Colonies. It was different in many ways from the New England Colonies. In New England, a half-million families, mostly of English descent, scratched out a living on small plots of rocky land. In contrast, fewer than 200,000 people lived in all of New York in 1776. Because of unusual land-grant policies, huge tracts of New York's fertile land were owned by a handful of men, most of them descended from the New World's early Dutch or English settlers. At the beginning of the American Revolution, then, about twenty wealthy families (including that of American General Philip Schuyler; 1733–1804) owned most of New York's land and wielded most of the region's political and economic power. These families were connected by intermarriage, and most of them—including many of the ordinary citizens of New York—were loyal to King George III (called Loyalists).

In 1776 New York City (the largest in the colony of New York) was nothing like the bustling city it is today. Its population then numbered about 25,000. (According to present-day estimates, about 7.5 million people now call the city home.) Most of the colonists in the prewar era lived on the southern tip

Map of the thirteeen colonies. *(XNR Productions. The Gale Group.)*

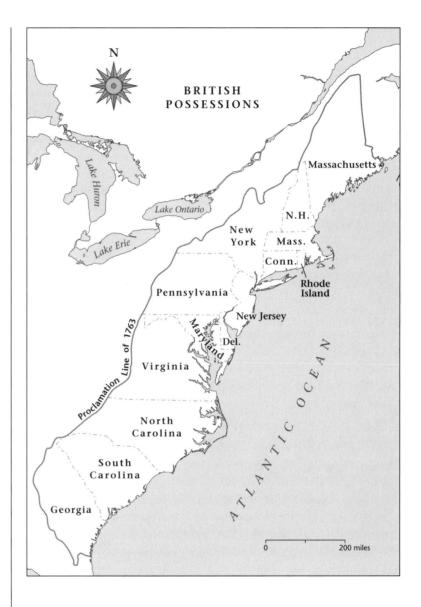

of a long, thin island called Manhattan. (Sometimes New York City is referred to simply as New York, and sometimes Manhattan—one of the five boroughs, or sections, of the city—is referred to as New York City. The other four boroughs of New York City are Staten Island, Brooklyn, the Bronx, and Queens.) New York's harbor bustled with shipping activity all year long, but the city still lagged behind Boston and Philadelphia in terms of shipping trade. What, then, was so important about New York that the British would set their sights on it?

The answer, in part, was New York's location and its status as a population center. Waterways were vital transportation routes in those days of poor roads. New York was situated on a lake-and-river chain that connected it with British-controlled Canada. Control of that chain meant control of the Hudson River. If Great Britain controlled the Hudson River, she could prevent the movement of American military supplies and soldiers and isolate New England and New York from the rest of the colonies. A country divided could be conquered more easily.

New York was also situated on a deep harbor that did not freeze in the winter. Soldiers could be transported to New York by ship at any time of the year, and British warships could easily anchor off New York. If the British wanted to take the colonies, they had to occupy every important center of strength; New York was such a center.

At the beginning of the war in 1775, the British believed that they could end the revolutionary conflict quickly by administering one fierce military blow to Boston, where colonial resistance was strongest. But Britain's technical "victory" at Boston's Bunker Hill was, in reality, no victory at all—the loss of redcoat soldiers was too high, and the rebels had not been subdued. (See Chapter 6: Lexington, Concord, and the Organization of Colonial Resistance.)

When General George Washington (1732–1799) showed that America had the men, the will, and the weapons to put up a strong defense, British General William Howe (1729–1814) abandoned Boston and headed for Nova Scotia, Canada, where he planned to rest, await reinforcements, then travel with them and await more reinforcements in New York. (Howe had replaced Thomas Gage as commander of British forces.) With New York City as their command center, the British sought to defeat all thirteen American colonies.

Continental army prepares to defend New York

Knowing early that New York was a prime British target, back in June 1775 Washington had sent Schuyler there (it was Schuyler's home colony) to begin the huge job of organizing and commanding a New York–based army. The difficulties

In June 1775, Washington sent Philip Schuyler to New York, where he would begin the huge job of organizing and commanding a New York-based army. *(Reproduced by permission of Archive Photos, Inc.)*

Schuyler faced were the same as those that troubled Washington, but where Washington had succeeded, Schuyler more often failed. His problem stemmed in part from an old boundary dispute that had pitted him and the citizens of New York (called "Yorkers") against New Englanders. Remembering their old hostility, "Yankee" volunteers from New England fought with Schuyler's "Yorker" soldiers; both groups were alienated by Schuyler's arrogant personality. Schuyler suffered from rheumatic (pronounced ROO-matic) gout, a hereditary and painful disease of the joints. His ill health kept him isolated and unable to attend to the needs of his men.

On top of the tension between Yankees and Yorkers, there was tension between New York's patriots and Loyalists. Patriot mobs enjoyed roughing up Loyalists in the streets. The Loyalist governor of New York, William Tryon (1729–1788), had become so nervous that in October of 1775, he took refuge on a British warship and stayed there for six months.

In January 1776, Washington sent General Charles Lee (1731–1782) to recruit volunteers in Connecticut for the defense of New York City. (Like Schuyler, Lee also suffered from gout—so badly that he had to be carried into New York City.) According to Mark M. Boatner III in *Encyclopedia of the American Revolution,* when Lee saw what kind of city New York was, he wrote to Washington: "What to do with the city, I [must say], puzzles me. It is so encircled with deep navigable waters [waters deep enough to allow ships through] that whoever commands the sea must command the town." This presented the colonists with a major problem, since America had no navy to speak of. Another major problem was the outrageous behavior of the men who had come to defend New York. Once again, it would become clear to George Washington that America's was not a trained and willing army.

Washington tries to control his men

Washington arrived in New York City on April 13, 1776, half expecting to find that Howe had gotten there ahead of him. He found the city poorly fortified, but he was equally dismayed by the soldiers who greeted him. The Americans were amateurs at soldiering, and they had mixed reasons for being there. Their motives ranged from patriotism to adventure and beyond, and many had never been away from home before. Richard Wheeler wrote in *Voices of 1776:* "Many of the men caused the general grief. They swam in the nude under the eyes of sensitive female citizens, they drank too much, fought ... [and] swore with such abandon that Washington began to fear that these insults to Heaven might affect the army's luck."

As he had done at Boston, Washington exerted the force of his personality and put his men to work. Over the next several months, he struggled to transform his men into something resembling professional soldiers. As Boatner put it: "The Americans dug like prairie dogs, throwing up numerous fortifications in and around New York City."

The call for independence

While Washington was bracing for an attack by the British in New York City, talk of independence swept across the colonies. Founding Father John Adams predicted: "Every day rolls in upon us Independence like a torrent." And on June 7, 1776, a clear call for independence was heard in Philadelphia. Congressman Richard Henry Lee (of the old and distinguished Lee family of Virginia) stood before Congress and read his bold proclamation, which began: "Resolved, That these United Colonies are, and of right ought to be, free and independent States, that they are absolved from all allegiance to the British Crown, and that all political connection between them and the State of Great Britain is, and ought to be, totally dissolved."

Next came a heated debate over this resolution. Most, but not all, of the delegates in Congress were in favor of independence. When no agreement could be reached, action on Lee's resolution was postponed for three weeks.

Drafting a Declaration of Independence

On June 11, 1776, the Continental Congress elected
Thomas Jefferson of Virginia (1743–1826), John Adams of
Massachusetts (1735–1826), Benjamin Franklin of Pennsylvania (1706–1790), Roger Sherman of Connecticut (1721–1793),
and Robert R. Livingston of New York (1746–1813)—known as
the Committee of Five—to draw up a statement that would present to the entire world the colonies' case for independence.
The resulting statement was the Declaration of Independence.

John Adams, a champion of independence, was elated
at Congress's move. As the Committee of Five went about its
work, Adams dominated it by the force of his personality. He
decided that Jefferson should draft the declaration. Many years
later, Adams explained his choice in a letter to his friend, Tim-
othy Pickering. Jefferson "had the Reputation of a masterly
Pen," wrote Adams. Up until that time, the shy, thirty-three-
year-old Jefferson had not spoken "three Sentences together"
in Congress. He disliked public speaking—apparently his voice

was weak—but he was well read and an eloquent writer. Jefferson hesitated to take on the enormous task; he thought that Adams ought to write the Declaration, but Adams felt he could not because he was too "unpopular."

Jefferson's document, with only a few changes made by the rest of the Committee, was presented to Congress for consideration on July 2, 1776. The Declaration of Independence offered the reasons why a separation from Great Britain was necessary (the three main reasons were taxation without representation, the presence of British troops in the colonies, and the trade restrictions imposed on the colonies by King George III and Parliament), and it laid out the truths for which the Revolutionary War was fought. The document was, in effect, a formal announcement by thirteen formerly separate colonies that they now considered themselves to be an independent and united nation. "With the signing [of the Declaration of Independence]," noted Edward F. Dolan in *The American Revolution: How We Fought the War of Independence,* "the thirteen British colonies ceased to exist." The purpose of the patriots' fight was to establish a new kind of nation—one in which men were entitled to "life, liberty and the pursuit of happiness." John Adams foresaw what a terrible war it would be when he wrote to a friend: "A bloody conflict we are destined to endure."

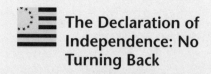

The Declaration of Independence: No Turning Back

The Declaration of Independence was read to a gathering of people in New York on July 9, 1776. The enthusiastic crowd of patriots who heard it reacted by tearing down the lead statue of King George III that stood in Bowling Green, New York (a green is a grassy gathering place). According to one estimate, the lead was later turned into 42,000 bullets for use by patriot soldiers.

Although the Declaration of Independence is regarded as a sacred document of American history, its original purpose was highly practical. Members of Congress believed that foreign countries would be unwilling to offer much-needed military assistance if America engaged in a civil war (a war between regions of the same nation). A war between two independent nations, however, would be an entirely different matter. Although there had been no official declaration of war by July of 1776, the world's first truly political war had begun. France and Spain—Great Britain's longtime enemies—could freely offer their assistance to the now independent United States of America.

The debate over independence

Long after the event, both John Adams and Thomas Jefferson wrote accounts of the congressional debates of July 1–4,

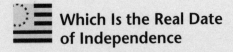

Which Is the Real Date of Independence

Richard Henry Lee's famous resolution—"That these United Colonies are, and of right ought to be, free and independent States"—sparked considerable controversy in Congress. On July 2, 1776, the resolution was passed; those in favor of a break with England had finally changed the minds of those who were opposed to it. As far as Congress was concerned, this was the most important event in the month of July. As John Adams wrote to his wife, Abigail, on July 3: "Yesterday, the greatest question was decided which ever was debated in America, and a greater, perhaps, never was nor will be decided among men."

It is interesting to note, however, that the United States does not celebrate the passage of Lee's resolution as a date of historic importance. Rather, July 4—the day Thomas Jefferson's Declaration of Independence was adopted—is commemorated as a national holiday known as Independence Day.

1776. The first matter up for discussion was Lee's resolution, which declared the colonies' independence. After much persuasive talk, the resolution was adopted by Congress on July 2, 1776. Then, Jefferson's Declaration of Independence was discussed at length. Jefferson decided to play a passive role in the debate, but he grew uncomfortable as he listened to Congress analyze each and every word of his document. Deliberation continued on July 3 and went over to the fourth. To distract the over-anxious Jefferson, Benjamin Franklin entertained him with amusing stories. John Adams led the fight for the adoption of the Declaration. As noted by Henry Steele Commager and Richard B. Morris in *The Spirit of Seventy-Six: The Story of the American Revolution as Told by Participants,* Jefferson wrote: "I will say for Mr. Adams, that he supported the Declaration with zeal and ability, fighting fearlessly for every word of it."

The Declaration of Independence was finally adopted later on July 4, nearly word for word as Jefferson had submitted it. As noted in *The John Adams Papers,* John Adams summed up the event this way: "I am well aware of the toil and blood and treasure it will cost us to maintain this declaration and support and defend these States. Yet through all the gloom I can see the rays of ravishing [dazzling; stunning] light and glory. I can see that the end is more than worth all the means, and that posterity [those who come after] will triumph in that day's transactions."

Declared: "All men are created equal"; blacks and women excluded

Some of the most stirring and often-repeated words from the Declaration of Independence are these: "We hold these truths to be self-evident, that all men are created equal...." (Self-evident truths are truths that require no proof or explanation.) The Declaration of Independence was a unique document for its time. The idea of all men being equal was a bold one, as was the notion that governments derive their powers from the consent of the men who are governed. But what about people of color? What about women?

Certainly there were many people who opposed slavery in 1776. In fact, Jefferson's original version of the Declaration of Independence contained a passage attacking slavery, even though Jefferson himself was a slave owner. But other slave-owning congressmen objected to this section of the document, so it was dropped.

The issue of the equality of women was not addressed in the Declaration of Independence, either. Abigail Adams (1744–1818), wife of Congressman John Adams, was a dedicated letter writer like her husband. He knew her thoughts on the topic of women's rights; back in 1775, she had voiced her opinion on the topic in one of her many letters to him. As quoted in "Women's Voices: Quotations from Women: Abigail Adams:"

Abigail Adams wrote to her husband John, asking him to "remember the ladies" while drafting the Declaration of Independence.
(Reproduced by permission of Archive Photos, Inc.)

> *In the new code of laws which I suppose it will be necessary for you to make, I desire you would remember the ladies and be more generous and favorable to them than your ancestors. Do not put such unlimited power into the hands of the husbands. Remember, all men would be tyrants if they could. If particular care and attention is not paid to the ladies, we are determined to foment [stir up] a rebellion, and will not hold ourselves bound by any laws in which we have no voice or representation.*

The Declaration of Independence was not a perfect document, principally because it excluded many people from its guarantees of equality. But signing it was an extremely courageous act. The fifty-five men who put their signatures on the historic document risked their lives and their property in doing so.

In June 1776, William Howe led three ships and 9,000 men to the peninsula of Sandy Hook at the mouth of lower New York Bay. *(Reproduced by permission of Archive Photos, Inc.)*

On July 4, 1776, church bells rang out over Philadelphia to announce the passage of the Declaration of Independence. But the actual signing of the Declaration by most members of the Continental Congress did not take place until August 2. The names of the signers, who were committing an act of treason in the eyes of the British, were kept secret until the following January, when American victories at Trenton and Princeton, New Jersey, made Congress bold enough to publish them.

Howe arrives in New York

While the Continental Congress was making historic decisions about a free and independent future for the colonies, Howe and his British troops were sailing for New York from Halifax, Nova Scotia. In June 1776, Howe led three ships and 9,000 men to the peninsula of Sandy Hook at the mouth of lower New York Bay. By the end of the month, he was joined by his brother, Admiral Richard Howe, who came from England with more ships and thousands of German soldiers (Hessians; pronounced HESH-uns). On July 2, 1776, the day the Declaration of Independence went before Congress for approval, General Howe landed his troops on Staten Island in New York harbor. Howe's ships met no opposition from the Americans.

Next, as New York patriots were celebrating the Declaration of Independence, the Howe brothers did something odd. Although they had orders to crush the rebellion in the colonies, they decided, in Richard Howe's words, to show "the people of America that the Door was yet open for Reconciliation." Both Howes had strong ties to the colonies. Their brother, George, had given his life to defend America during the French and Indian War (1756–63), and the grateful citizens of Massachusetts erected a monument in his honor. What was more, the Howes were sympathetic to the American cause. Their behavior during the Revolutionary War still has historians debating about whether they really wanted to win it for the British.

On July 14, 1776, the Howes sent a letter addressed to George Washington, Esquire. ("Esquire" is a courtesy title, roughly equivalent to "Mr. George Washington.") According to James Thomas Flexner's *George Washington in the American Revolution (1775–1783)*, Washington's assistants informed the British messenger that "there was no such person in the army.... If Lord Howe wishes to communicate with *General Washington* [emphasis added], he must address him properly." The Howes could not do that because the British government refused to recognize Washington's post in the Continental army. When Washington finally agreed to a meeting with the Howes' representative, Colonel Paterson, he learned that the British were offering to "pardon" the rebel colonists, meaning they would forgive the Americans for their defiance and disloyalty. Washington replied that "those who had committed no fault [needed] no pardon."

A week later, Colonel Henry Knox (1750–1806), who was present at the meeting between Paterson and Washington, wrote to his wife, Lucy: "General Washington was very handsomely dressed and made a most elegant appearance. Paterson appeared awe-struck, as if he was before something supernatural. Indeed I don't wonder at it. He was before a very great man indeed." Both Washington and the Continental Congress rejected the Howes' offer. The Howes felt they were left with no choice but to use military force to make the Americans change their minds.

Howe has trouble with reinforcements

But the Howes were not yet in a position to attack; they were still waiting for the rest of the reinforcements that trickled into New York throughout the summer. The new soldiers came from England, Scotland, Germany, and parts of the British Empire. Some were former black slaves, all that was left of Lord Dunmore's Ethiopian Regiment after most were killed in battle or by disease (see Chapter 8: Native Americans and Blacks in the American Revolution). Britain's forces came on ships escorted by men-of-war (warships) to protect them and their supplies from raids by American privateers. (Privateers are privately owned ships authorized by governments to attack and capture enemy vessels during wartime.) A sizeable number of Loyalist citizens of New York also volunteered to serve under William Howe.

Howe was greeted warmly and enjoyed a comfortable few months gambling, dining, and entertaining the ladies of New York. But, like Washington, Howe did not have an easy time with his troops. Although they were disciplined, professional soldiers, they were restless from lack of activity and anxious to engage the despised American soldiers in battle. One of Howe's officers, Francis Rawdon-Hastings (known as Lord Rawdon), summed up the situation in a letter to a friend in England. Rawdon's letter, excerpted in Henry Steele Commager and Richard B. Morris's *Spirit of Seventy-Six: The Story of the American Revolution as Told by Participants* and reprinted in part here, was dated August 5, 1776:

> The fair nymphs of this isle are in [big trouble], as the fresh meat our men have got here [supplied by New York farmers] has made them ... riotous.... Some of the Hessians [German soldiers] have arrived and long [want] much to have a brush with the rebels, of whom they have a most despicable [low and hateful] opinion. They are good troops but ... nothing equal to ours. I imagine that we shall very soon come to action, and I do not doubt but the consequence will be fatal to the rebels. An army composed as theirs is cannot bear the frown of adversity [cannot survive hardship].

British reinforcements continued to flow in, and by August 12, 1776, William Howe had about 33,000 soldiers at Staten Island. His brother, Richard Howe, supported him with 10 "ships of the line" (ships large enough to contain 74 or more guns), 20 frigates (high-speed warships) with a total of 1,200 guns, hundreds of smaller ships, and 10,000 seaman. The Howes, at the head of the largest force England had ever sent overseas, were ready to test the strength of the American army, whom they outnumbered by about two to one. William Howe planned to invade Long Island later in the month.

Howe takes New York City

By August 19, Washington had been able to collect 23,000 soldiers, who were more or less trained for duty and

Both Washington and Howe prepared for battle in New York.
(Reproduced by permission of Corbis Corporation [Bellevue].)

were strung out all along the waterways around New York City. They were poorly armed and equipped and unsupported by navy, cavalry (soldiers on horseback), or artillery (soldiers who operate weapons such as cannons that throw projectiles [bombs] across the field of battle). Hundreds of soldiers were afflicted with the diseases that plagued army camps throughout the war.

Washington knew from the size of the British force confronting him that Great Britain now took the Americans very seriously. A dreadful phase of the war was about to begin. Washington was short of trained men and experienced officers; some were sick, and some were defending other parts of the country. William Howe believed that if Washington were a gentleman, he would surrender at once. A British general would never engage in a battle unless he were reasonably sure he could win. Washington had little hope for a victory. Historians continue to argue over his decision to try to defend New York. One theory is that Washington and Congress felt it would reflect poorly on the American cause to simply hand the city over to the British without a fight.

Preparations for the attack on New York began the third week of August. In the middle of a torrential rainstorm, 20,000 of Howe's troops crossed the narrow channel from Staten Island to Long Island. There they joined in battle with Washington's 12,000 troops, ferried over from New York City. The next day, as the fighting raged, Washington wrote to Congress:

> I trust, through divine favor and our own exertions [the British] will be disappointed in their [objectives], and, at all events, any advantages they may gain will cost them very dear. If our troops will behave well ... they will have to wade through much blood and slaughter ... and at best be possessed of a melancholy and mournful victory. May the sacredness of our cause inspire our soldier[s] with sentiments of heroism. (Washington in J. T. Flexner, George Washington in the American Revolution, p. 106)

By August 27, 1776, the outcome of the Battle of Long Island had been decided: America's forces were soundly beaten. The British then pursued the Americans across the East River to Manhattan, where Washington held out against them for two months, despite horrible living conditions and the constant, menacing threat of Howe's superior forces.

Washington calls out the submarine

Trapped in Manhattan, Washington's men were dejected by their humiliating defeat on Long Island. Supplies were low, the weather was terrible (wet tents, blankets, and clothing were draped everywhere), the men were tired, and they had lost confidence in their leaders. With bitterness, they began to desert, taking their weapons with them. According to Captain Alexander Graydon of Philadelphia, as quoted in Wheeler's *Voices of 1776:* "A greater loss than themselves was that of the arms and ammunition they took away with them.... It was found necessary to post a guard ... to stop the fugitives; and ... upon one of them being arrested with a number of *notions* [odds and ends] in a bag, there was found among them a cannon ball which, he said, he was taking home to his mother for the purpose of pounding mustard [seeds]."

The British troops on Long Island and the American troops on Manhattan entertained themselves by looting and vandalizing abandoned homes, orchards, and vegetable gar-

Spies in the Revolution

One of George Washington's first large expenditures after he was made commander in chief of the Continental army in the summer of 1775 was for someone "to go into the town of Boston to establish secret correspondence." (This cost him $333.33.) Thus did Washington set up his own "secret service." Washington's spies mingled with British soldiers and reported back from taverns and coffeehouses, providing him with intelligence about what was going on in Boston. He learned that Boston had no fresh food; that milk cows were being slaughtered for beef because there was nothing to feed them; and that fuel was scarce. From this information, Washington deduced that the British must be planning either to sail away from Boston or give up the fight. (Actually, William Howe was just waiting for reinforcements from England.)

As Washington sat in New York in the fall of 1776, wondering what the enemy was up to, he ordered spies sent to Long Island. One of the first to volunteer was twenty-four-year-old Nathan Hale. Disguised as a schoolteacher (his former occupation), Hale penetrated the enemy camp and gathered the information Washington wanted, but he was captured during the trip back to his own camp. Howe ordered Hale hanged without a trial. And so he was, on September 22, 1776. His last words were, "I only regret that I have but one life to lose for my country."

Spies sometimes carried messages inside of hollow, silver bullets, which they could swallow if they were captured. The "Silver Bullet Trick" was a special favorite of British spies. The most famous British spy was Major John André (1750–1780), who played an important part in getting the American traitor Benedict Arnold (1741–1801; formerly a distinguished officer in the Continental army and a close ally of General Washington) to go over to the British side. Like Nathan Hale, André was captured and hanged. Also like Hale, André was mourned by both sides because of the brave way he accepted his fate.

dens. Washington ordered a roll call three times a day to try and stop the mayhem. He watched British warships sail up and down the rivers on both sides of Manhattan Island and contemplated his next move. Then, he decided to call upon a young man by the name of David Bushnell.

Bushnell was a perfect example of a quality called "Yankee ingenuity." That was a term used by admiring American backwoodsmen and plantation dwellers to describe travel-

"There was a great deal of plundering..."

To the disgust of colonial citizens, as British and Hessian soldiers marched through New York and New Jersey in 1776–1777, they shot prisoners and ransacked villages and towns. It was said that they burned houses, cut down fruit trees, killed sheep, plundered and stole, and molested young girls and women. Eventually, the Continental Congress appointed a committee to investigate the charges. As reprinted in Frank Moore's *Diary of the American Revolution,* Congress reported in part: "[T]he whole track of the British army is marked with desolation and a wanton destruction of property.... [P]risoners, instead of that humane treatment which those taken by the United States experienced, were in general treated with the greatest barbarity.... [T]he committee had authentic information of many instances of the most indecent treatment ... of married and single women..." The committee concluded: "The cry of barbarity and cruelty is but too well founded ... [and] filled this whole continent with resentment and horror."

Johannes Reuber (pronounced yo-HANN-iss ROO-ber) was one of the Hessians taken prisoner at Trenton, New Jersey, in 1776 and marched to Philadelphia. (See subhead in this chapter titled "Washington's desperate move.") Reuber recorded in his diary interesting details about George Washington's treatment of Hessian prisoners. The following quote was excerpted by William H. Dwyer in *The Day Is Ours!:*

> General Washington of the Americans made a proclamation and it was posted all over the city: the Hessians were without blame and had been forced into this war. The Hessians had not come of their own free will. They should not be regarded as enemies but as friends of the American people and should be treated as such.

ing New England peddlers who made and sold clever gadgets. As a student at Yale University (in Connecticut) from 1771 to 1775, the young Bushnell had demonstrated to his unbelieving instructors that gunpowder could be exploded underwater. By the time Washington called upon him in 1776, Bushnell had managed to put together a working submarine. His *American Turtle,* so-called because it resembled two joined turtle shells, was sent to attack the British ship *Cerberus.* The attack failed when the *Turtle*'s operator could not overcome technical difficulties and make his weapon explode. The public laughed back then, but modern versions of Bushnell's submarine are

Because General Washington had full authority and he gave his honest word, it became better for us [we were treated better]. All day long, Americans big and little, rich and poor, came to the barracks and brought food to us and treated us with kindness and humanity.

It is interesting to note that 5,000 of the nearly 30,000 German soldiers who came to America deserted their posts in the British army; many received permission at the end of the war to remain in America.

British Parliament eventually conducted an inquiry into the plunder of New York and New Jersey by British forces. A witness named General James Robertson seemed to blame the German soldiers for most of the misconduct. According to Charles Francis Adams in a *Massachusetts Historical Society Proceedings* article, Robertson responded in part: "There was a great deal of plundering.... I saw some men hanged, by Sir William Howe's orders, for plundering; and I have heard that after Mr. Washington took the Hessians at Trenton, he restored to the inhabitants [of Trenton] twenty-one waggon-loads of plunder he had found among their baggage...."

But it was not just the British and Hessians who were guilty of looting and plundering. American soldiers took their turn as well. New Jersey citizens were so appalled at the disgraceful behavior of Washington's deserting soldiers in the winter of 1776–1777 that thousands flocked to British camps to swear allegiance to the king. In *George Washington and the American Revolution* Burke Davis noted that "about five thousand New Jersey civilians trooped into British camps to take an oath of allegiance."

now standard naval weapons. (The U.S. Army recognized Bushnell's talent, though, and he went on to enjoy a distinguished career with the military.)

The British capture New York

On September 8, 1776, Washington wrote to Congress from his headquarters in New York: "It is now extremely obvious, from all Intelligence [spies' reports; see box titled "Spies in the Revolution"], that having landed their whole Army on Long-Island, (except about 4,000 on Staten-Island) [the

British] mean to enclose us on the Island of New-York." Facing an army of superior numbers and greater discipline than his own, Washington recommended that New York be abandoned to the British. On September 14, Congress replied that Washington should not "remain in that city a moment longer than he shall think it proper."

On September 15, before Washington could evacuate it, Howe attacked Manhattan. As his troops swarmed ashore, cannons were discharged from the ships that carried them. The American rebels deserted the town in a great, confused rush. Washington tried to rally his troops, riding his horse back and forth among them and threatening them with sword and pistol. In disgust, he is said to have thrown down his hat and cried: "Are these the men with which I am to defend America?"

Shortly after midnight on September 20, 1776, as Washington and his men were retreating northward and the British were settling down in Manhattan, a fire broke out in the city. Before citizens and British soldiers could put out the flames, 493 houses were destroyed. The British claimed Washington's troops had set the fire, but this has never been proven. New York City would serve as headquarters for the British army for the rest of the Revolutionary War.

Early October found the American navy fighting a losing battle against the superior British fleet on Lake Champlain (a lake that separates New York from Vermont and extends into Canada). Then, the British under Howe attacked the American ground troops at White Plains, New York, on October 28,1776. It had taken Howe two months from the time he took Long Island to drive Washington up to White Plains—a distance of less than thirty miles. Many historians suggest that Howe hesitated too often and failed to take the offensive when he should have. If he had moved faster and with more firmness during the New York campaign, he may well have destroyed the American army and won the war. Instead, the fighting would drag on for five more years.

Washington retreats across New Jersey

Washington stationed men at forts in New York and New Jersey while he retreated westward across New Jersey

Within the map:

N

New York

Hudson R.

Peekskill

Oct. 28, 1776

White Plains

Delaware River

Nov. 16, 1776

New Jersey

Howe

Fort Lee

Fort Washington

Morristown

Washington

New York

Aug. 27, 1776

Washington

Long Island

Cornwallis

Dec. 25, 1776: Washington leads his force of 2,400 men across the Delaware River.

Staten Island

Sandy Hook

General Howe

Admiral Howe

Princeton

Jan. 3, 1777

Clinton

ATLANTIC OCEAN

Trenton

Dec. 27, 1776

Pennsylvania

Delaware River

0   20 miles

→ American advance
--→ American retreat
→ British advance
--→ British retreat
✸ American victory
✸ British victory

with the main body of the army. This meant that his army, small to begin with, was now divided. The result of this division was tragedy. A group under the command of young General Nathanael Greene (1742–1786) made a last New York stand at Manhattan's Fort Washington on November 16, 1776, and 2,800 American troops were taken prisoner. This was one of the costliest battles of the entire war, and it dealt the American cause a staggering blow.

British and German soldiers then pursued Greene and his remaining troops across the Hudson River to Fort Lee, New Jersey. The British took the fort on November 20. Greene and his men fled "like scared rabbits," according to one British officer, to join Washington at Hackensack. From there, the American army began a retreat southward through New Jersey, all the while pursued by British troops under Major General Charles Cornwallis (1738–1805). The pattern of American retreats reflected Washington's concerns about losing his army. To Washington, "The army was the Revolution," asserted Albert Marrin in *The War for Independence: The Story of the American Revolution.* "He would never risk the army's destruction, for fear of destroying the Revolution along with it." It was during the engagements in New Jersey that Cornwallis made his often-quoted remark that he would capture Washington like a hunter "bags" a fox.

Judge Thomas Jones (1731–1792) wrote the only history of the American Revolution from the point of view of a Loyalist who was there. In it—as excerpted in Wheeler's *Voices of 1776*—he described the state of the American army in November 1776: "[They were] half-starved, half-clothed, half-armed, discontented, ungovernable, undisciplined wretches." A poor army they might be, but they were all Washington had. Unfortunately, their terms of duty were due to expire at the end of December.

Crossing the Delaware

The Continental army's retreat took a westward turn toward the Delaware River, which forms the border between New Jersey and Pennsylvania. "Cornwallis snapped at [Washington's] heels," commented Dolan in *The American Revolution.* "To delay the Britisher's wagons and artillery, the Americans burned every bridge they crossed and sent one tree after another toppling across the roadway with their axes." In early December, Washington finally crossed the Delaware into Pennsylvania. With him were 2,000 troops, all that remained of his original force of about 20,000 men. Soldiers had deserted by the thousands after the string of humiliating losses in New York. With his reputation severely damaged by the fall of New York, Washington managed to pick up only a few new volunteers in New Jersey, and he did not expect a good turnout in Pennsylvania, either. He faced the darkest hour of the Revolutionary War up to that time, although things would get worse. The American

general summed up the circumstances in a letter to his brother Lund: "[Y]our imagination can scarce extend to a situation more distressing than mine.... I think the game is pretty near up."

As Washington was crossing the Delaware, Howe stationed men at several posts from New York City to Trenton and Bordentown, New Jersey. Then, on December 13, Howe announced that he was finished making war for the winter season—a common practice among professional soldiers of the period. Howe planned to move on to Philadelphia in the spring of 1777. According to military historian T. Harry Williams in *The History of American Wars from 1745 to 1918*, if Howe had moved on immediately, "he undoubtedly could have taken Philadelphia, the largest city in [eighteenth-century] America and, as the seat of Congress, the capital. He might also have taken the little American army or at least dispersed [scattered] it, and the blow possibly would have destroyed the rebel will to continue the war. He was satisfied, however, with what he had accomplished."

General Washington and his troops prepare to cross the Delaware River into Pennsylvania.
(Reproduced by permission of Corbis Corporation [Bellevue].)

Congress Flees to Baltimore

After driving the American army out of New York, the British were "so proud and sure of success," according to George Washington, that they decided to push on to Philadelphia, home base of the Continental Congress. "I have positive information that this is a fact," wrote Washington to General Charles Lee. "Should they now really risk this undertaking then there is a great probability that they will pay dearly for it for I shall continue to retreat before them so as to lull them into security." At this point, Washington did not know that Howe did not plan such a move until spring.

When members of Congress heard that a unit of the British army was in Trenton, New Jersey (thirty-five miles away), they decided it would be wise to relocate to Baltimore, Maryland, a distance of about 110 miles from Philadelphia. They made the move on December 12, 1776. According to delegate General Oliver Wolcott (1726–1797), the relocation was necessary because "it was judged that the Council of America ought not to sit in a place liable to be interrupted by the rude disorder of arms."

During this upheaval, Washington complained that Congress, always too slow to act, would be even slower if they were farther away. He predicted that in ten more days, his army would no longer exist unless something drastic were done. Congress adopted a resolution after they "maturely considered the present crisis" and gave Washington broad powers to raise a new army.

Only about two dozen members of Congress showed up in Baltimore.

Meanwhile, 1,500 Hessian soldiers under the command of fifty-five-year-old Colonel Johann Gottlieb Rall (pronounced YO-hahn GOTT-leeb RAWL; 1720–1776) settled in for the winter at Trenton, a village of about a hundred scattered houses at the falls of the Delaware River. Rall was a loud, hard-drinking man who spoke no English and held American soldiers in low regard. (He referred to them contemptibly as "nothing but a lot of farmers.") Rall's attitude carried over to his men, who had so little regard for American soldiers and their attack power that they built no fortifications. They were confident that even such an ungentlemanly bunch as the Americans would not engage in battle during the Christmas season.

(Congress remained in Baltimore for three months, until after Washington defeated the British in New Jersey.) Historians have criticized Congress for its actions during the war years, especially during the crisis of December 1776, when they seemed to be fleeing from Philadelphia to save their own skins. In their panic, they left the whole burden of defending America to one man—George Washington. But historian Lynn Montross defended the Continental Congress. Montross pointed out the tremendous personal sacrifices made by members of Congress throughout the war. They faced death by hanging if the war for independence were lost. Montross wrote: "Before the war ended, more than half of the members were fated to have their property looted or destroyed. Others were to be imprisoned or driven into hiding by man hunts, and even their families would not escape persecution." Furthermore, "the statistics of the Continental Congress show a record of military service which has probably never been bettered by any other [governing body] of history. Of the 342 men elected during the fifteen years, 134 bore arms in either the militia or the Continental army. One was killed in action, twelve seriously wounded, and twenty-three taken prisoners in combat. When it is recalled that a majority of the delegates had passed the age of 40, the valor of Congress needs no apologies."

Primary source for the excerpt from Washington's letter to General Charles Lee, which Lee never received, and which was found in some papers in Germany: William S. Stryker, The Battles of Trenton and Princeton. *Boston and New York: Houghton, Mifflin, 1898, pp. 326–27. Primary source for the excerpt from Wolcott's letter to his wife: Henry P. Johnston,* The Campaign of 1776 around New York and Brooklyn.... *Brooklyn: Long Island Historical Society, 1878, pp. 147–48.*

Washington's desperate move

At this point in time—in December 1776— Washington was truly a desperate man. Even though the war for independence seemed on the verge of collapse, he needed to convince the American people that the revolutionary cause was still alive. He also needed to rally his dejected army, or he could not count on anyone signing up again for service. Just when the situation looked completely hopeless, Thomas Paine—the author of *Common Sense* (see Chapter 3: Literature and the Arts in the Revolutionary Era)—sent a famous and inspiring message to Washington's miserable men: "These are the times that try men's souls," he wrote in his newest pamphlet. "The harder the conflict, the more glorious the triumph."

By the end of December, Washington had reinforcements, including the men who had served under General Lee. (Charles Lee, an English-born major general in the Continental army, was captured by the British on December 13 while on his way to join Washington. A harsh critic of Washington, Lee would later try unsuccessfully to help the British win the war. He was dismissed from the American army in 1780.) Washington's troop strength was now up to 6,000. On December 25, 1776, in freezing sleet and rain, he led a force of 2,400 men back across the Delaware River north of Philadelphia. They marched to Trenton and surrounded the town as the 1,500 Hessians lay sleeping off the ill effects of their Christmas celebrations. Colonel Henry Knox described the taking of Trenton in a letter to his wife dated December 28, 1776:

> *The floating ice in the river made the labor almost incredible.... The night was cold and stormy; it hailed with great violence; the troops marched with the most profound silence and good order.... The storm continued with great violence, but was in our backs, and consequently in the faces of our enemy. About half a mile from the town was [a party of soldiers guarding Trenton]. These we forced, and entered the town with them pell-mell [in disorder and confusion]; and here succeeded a scene of war of which I had often conceived, but never saw before.*

> *The hurry, fright and confusion of the enemy was [not] unlike that which will be when the last trump[et] shall sound [signaling the end of the world]. [At last] they were driven through the town into an open plain.... [T]he poor fellows ... saw themselves completely surrounded.... The Hessians lost part of the cannon in the town ... and were obliged to surrender upon the spot.... The number of prisoners was above 1,200 including officers—all Hessians [other sources claim between 920 and 1,000 men surrendered]. There were few killed or wounded on either side [perhaps 25 killed, 90 wounded].... Providence [God] seemed to have smiled upon every part of this enterprise.*

Rall was killed in the conflict. Among those captured was a twenty-five-piece band. The band went with the other prisoners to Philadelphia, and when that city celebrated the first anniversary of independence seven months later, the German band provided the music. Washington called the victory "a glorious day for our country."

Patriot morale restored; Washington proclaimed a hero

On January 3, 1777, Washington followed up his stunning success at Trenton by taking Princeton, New Jersey. He

then retired for the winter at Morristown, New Jersey. The British enemy had been pushed out of most parts of the state. Howe would soon resign as commander in chief of British forces in America, complaining that the British government had failed to send him enough reinforcements.

Washington remained in Morristown for almost five months. On March 14, 1777, he reported to Congress that he had fewer than 3,000 men, and they were suffering the ravaging effects of starvation and smallpox.

Elsewhere, a new spirit of optimism was unfolding. As news spread of Washington's achievements at Trenton and Princeton, his reputation was restored. Nicholas Cresswell, an Englishman traveling in America (see Chapter 7: Assembling an Army [1775–1776]), was in Leesburg, Virginia, when he heard the news. He recorded in his diary: "Six weeks ago [my host] was lamenting the unhappy situation of the Americans and pitying the wretched condition of their much-beloved

The Hessians surrender to Washington and his troops, after the Battle of Trenton.
(Reproduced by permission of Archive Photos, Inc.)

Treatment of Sick and Wounded Soldiers

Smallpox killed more soldiers during the American Revolution than did enemy soldiers. John Adams once remarked: "Disease has destroyed ten men for us where the sword of the enemy has killed one." George Washington's army faced its first major bout with smallpox while in Morristown during the winter of 1777. Smallpox causes fever, vomiting, skin eruptions, and sometimes death, and it is easily passed to others. The disease spread so rapidly that Washington was forced to turn Morristown homes into hospital rooms. There (according to Burke Davis in *George Washington and the American Revolution*) he conducted what was probably the first mass inoculation against smallpox in American history. Inoculation for smallpox involved injecting the disease virus into the body to cause a minor form of the disease so that a person could build up protection against it.

Both British and American soldiers had a deep-seated fear of hospitals. In fact, it was widely believed that the battlefield was a less dangerous place than an eighteenth-century hospital. Revolutionary-era hospitals were usually set up as needed in churches, town halls, or schoolhouses. They were always overcrowded, unsanitary, and short of medical supplies. The wounded were usually laid upon filthy piles of straw, bloodied by the soldiers who had already died on them.

Medical knowledge was scant, and surgeons were often ill-trained—or even untrained. Painkilling medication was unknown, so surgeons who operated on wounded soldiers usually gave their patients lead musket balls to bite or chew. (A musket was a type of shoulder gun; the balls were like bullets.) The balls kept the patient from crying out or biting his tongue when the painful surgery began. "Biting the bullet" today still means enduring suffering in silence.

Townspeople did not welcome hospitals set up near them. Patients were

General, supposing his [lack] of skill and experience in military matters had brought them all to the brink of destruction. In short, all was gone, all was lost. But now," Cresswell concluded, "the scale is turned and Washington's name is [praised] to the clouds."

Washington's triumph was also noted in Europe. As quoted in Robert Leckie's, *George Washington's War*, King Frederick the Great of Prussia (a former state in Germany), a bril-

often forced to leave as soon as they could walk. Even worse than these makeshift hospitals were British prison hospitals, where sick American prisoners of war were allowed to starve to death. Worst of all were British prison ships, where up to 500 American prisoners of war might be held on rotten, leaking vessels meant to hold no more than 100 people. Robert Leckie vividly described the situation facing Americans on board a typical British prison ship:

> Fed four moldy biscuits and a bit of rancid butter daily, with an occasional bit of meat and a canteen of water ... [they lay] below decks in their own filth or squeezed together gasping in the foul, fetid air, half naked and often delirious, ravished by smallpox or attacked by ghoulish guards wielding cutlasses [curved swords]. Their nights [were] made hideous by the piteous crying and groaning of the stricken, their days darkened by despair, freezing in winter in unheated holds and suffocating in summer in the airless dark. [T]hey died at the rate of four or five a day. Indeed, a quick death was their only hope, unless they chose to escape by serving King George.

In 1780 Philip Freneau (1752–1832) published his poem "The British Prison Ship." Freneau, called the poet of American independence and the father of American poetry, was a wealthy man who built and commanded a privateer, the *Aurora*. Privateers were privately owned ships that were authorized by Congress to attack and capture enemy vessels. They made up a large part of America's makeshift "navy" during the Revolutionary War. Freneau's ship was captured by the British in 1780, and he was imprisoned aboard the *Scorpion*. His health suffered from the ill treatment he received, and he was transferred to a British hospital ship, the *Hunter*. His poem recounts his terrible experiences on both ships. Freneau described the meat served to prisoners aboard the *Hunter* as "carrion [dead and rotting flesh] torn from hungry crows" with "vermin vile [disgusting maggots] on every joint."

liant soldier, exclaimed: "The achievements of Washington and his little band of compatriots ... were the most brilliant of any recorded in the history of military achievements." Even more gratifying was the reaction of France. Unwilling to join the American side while Washington was losing, with Washington a hero, the French attitude changed. Slowly, the French began supplying America with weapons. French troops would follow.

Stirred into a patriotic fervor by the words of Thomas

Paine and Washington's victories, America rallied anew to the cause of independence. New recruits signed up for the Continental army, and by summer Washington's forces numbered 9,000.

For More Information

Books

Boyd, Julian P. *The Declaration of Independence.* Princeton, NJ: Princeton University Press, 1945.

Diamant, Lincoln. *Yankee Doodle Days: Exploring the American Revolution.* Fleischmanns, NY: Purple Mountain, 1996.

Martin, Joseph Plumb. *Yankee Doodle Boy: A Young Soldier's Adventures in the American Revolution Told by Himself.* Reprinted. New York: Holiday House, 1995.

Web Sites

National Archives and Records Administration. "The Declaration of Independence." [Online] Available http://www.nara.gov/exhall/charters/declaration/decmain.html (accessed on February 9, 2000).

"Printed Ephemera: Three Centuries of Broadsides and Other Printed Ephemera." Including a Baltimore broadside of 1776 giving the first published account of George Washington crossing the Delaware. [Online] Available http://memory.loc.gov/ammem/rbpehtml/pehome.html (accessed on July 30, 1999).

Sources

Books

Boatner, Mark M. III. *Encyclopedia of the American Revolution.* Mechanicsburg, PA: Stackpole Books, 1994.

Commager, Henry Steele, and Richard B. Morris, eds. *The Spirit of Seventy-Six: The Story of the American Revolution as Told by Participants.* New York: Da Capo Press, 1995.

Cresswell, Nicholas. *The Journal of Nicholas Cresswell: 1774–1777.* London: Jonathan Cape, 1918.

Davis, Burke. *George Washington and the American Revolution.* New York: Random House, 1975.

Dolan, Edward F. *The American Revolution: How We Fought the War of Independence.* Brookfield, CT: Millbrook Press, 1995.

Donovan, Frank, ed. *The John Adams Papers.* New York: Dodd, Mead & Co., 1965.

Drake, Francis Samuel, and Henry Knox. *Life and Correspondence of Henry Knox, Major-General in the American Revolutionary Army.* Boston: S.G. Drake, 1873.

Dwyer, William H. *The Day Is Ours! November 1776–January 1777: An Inside View of the Battles of Trenton and Princeton.* New York: Viking Press, 1983.

Flexner, James Thomas. *George Washington in the American Revolution (1775–1783).* Boston: Little, Brown, 1968.

Gruber, Ira D. "Vain Hopes and Lost Opportunities." In *The Howe Brothers and the American Revolution.* New York: W.W. Norton, 1972, pp. 89–126.

Johnston, Henry P. *The Campaign of 1776 around New York and Brooklyn.* Brooklyn: Long Island Historical Society, 1878, pp. 147–48.

Leckie, Robert. *George Washington's War.* New York: HarperCollins, 1992.

Marrin, Albert. *The War for Independence: The Story of the American Revolution.* New York: Atheneum, 1988.

Millett, Allan R., and Peter Maslowski. *For the Common Defense: A Military History of the United States of America.* New York: The Free Press, 1984.

Montross, Lynn. *The Reluctant Rebels: The Story of the Continental Congress, 1774–1789.* New York: Harper & Bros., 1950.

Moore, Frank, ed. *Diary of the American Revolution. From Newspapers and Original Documents.* 2 vols. New York: Charles Scribner, 1860. Vol. 1, pp. 419–22.

Rhodehamel, John, ed. *George Washington, Writings.* New York: Literary Classics of the United States, Inc., 1997.

Stryker, William S. *The Battles of Trenton and Princeton.* Boston and New York: Houghton, Mifflin, 1898.

Wheeler, Richard. *Voices of 1776.* New York: Thomas Y. Crowell, 1972.

Williams, T. Harry. *The History of American Wars from 1745 to 1918.* New York: Alfred A. Knopf, 1981, pp. 3–82.

Wright, Esmond. "The New York Loyalists." In *The Loyalist Americans: A Focus on Greater New York.* Edited by Robert A. East and Jacob Judd. Tarrytown, NY: Sleepy Hollow Restorations, 1975.

Web Sites

"American Revolution Timeline: Conflict and Revolution, 1775–1776." The History Place. [Online] Available http://www.historyplace.com/ unitedstates/revolution/ revwar-75.htm (accessed on January 20, 2000).

"American Revolution Timeline: An Unlikely Victory, 1777–1783." The History Place. [Online] Available http://www.historyplace.com/ unitedstates/revolution/revwar-77.htm (accessed on January 20, 2000).

Mullin, James. "The Irish People: The Voice of Irish Republicanism in America. Philip Freneau, poet on the prison ship." [Online] Available http://inac.org/IrishPeople/top/12_26_98/122698mullin.html (accessed on August 10, 1999).

"Women's Voices: Quotations from Women: Abigail Adams." [Online] Available http://womenshistory.miningco.com/education/womenshistory/library/qu/blquadam.htm (accessed on February 17, 2000).

Other

Adams, Charles Francis. "Contemporary Opinion on the Howes." *Massachusetts Historical Society Proceedings,* XLIV, pp. 118–20.

The Crossing. An A&E Network and Columbia TriStar Television Production. Screenplay by Howard Fast, based on his novel of the same name; starring Jeff Daniels as George Washington. Broadcast premiere on A&E (Arts & Entertainment cable television network), January 10, 2000.

The Agonizing Path to Victory (1777–1778)

10

After capturing New York City, British General William Howe (1729–1814) set out to seize the Hudson River Valley and isolate New England from the rest of the colonies. His efforts kept George Washington (1732–1799), commander in chief of the Continental army, occupied in 1777 and 1778. Howe's mission was part of a three-pronged plan for British victory in America. The other two targets were Canada (a campaign handled by British generals Guy Carleton and John Burgoyne) and the Southern Colonies (a land and sea expedition planned for 1778–79 and headed by General Henry Clinton, who succeeded Howe as commander in chief of British forces in America in May 1778).

In January 1777, after his completely unexpected victories at Trenton and Princeton, New Jersey, George Washington had settled in for a miserably uncomfortable winter at Morristown, New Jersey. Meanwhile, Howe and his British troops enjoyed a comfortable winter in New York.

Washington was gratified to see his Continental army achieve its greatest strength in 1777–78, when it reached a total of about 35,000 men (not all of them were with Washington; some were in Canada and in the South). Late in 1776, the Continental Congress had authorized the raising of 76,000 troops, who would serve for three years or until the war ended. Formerly, soldiers were required to serve for just one year. As it turned out, though, nowhere near 76,000 troops ever actually served in America's army at once. Each state was given a quota—a number of soldiers it was required to provide—but none of the states ever met its quota.

America's prospects looked bright when, in the summer of 1777, Washington welcomed to his ranks a volunteer soldier from France. The nineteen-year-old Marquis (pronounced mar-KEE) de Lafayette (1757–1834) had come without the permission of his government. At this point in time, the French were still not sure about joining the Americans—who seemed to lose more often than they won—against the British. It would take another spectacular victory before France decided to enter the Revolutionary War.

Howe takes Philadelphia

Howe and Washington spent the spring and early summer of 1777 in minor skirmishes in New Jersey. Howe did not have enough troops to chase after Washington, and Washington's troop strength was down to 1,000 men, many of them sick. By the end of the summer, though, Washington had 8,000 new men. In late August, he rode at the side of his new friend and admirer, the Marquis de Lafayette, through the streets of Philadelphia, America's capital and General Howe's next target.

Around the same time, Howe landed his forces at the top of the Chesapeake Bay in northeastern Maryland. He planned to march through Delaware and into Pennsylvania, then take the all-important city of Philadelphia. Upon learning of Howe's intentions, Washington and his troops rushed to Brandywine Creek (on the Delaware-Pennsylvania border) and awaited Howe's arrival. Howe's troops proved stronger than Washington's; they succeeded in pushing the American soldiers northward. The Americans retreated toward Philadelphia, and the city fell to Howe's forces on September 26, 1777.

Like the loss of New York City, the capture of what was then America's largest city was another embarrassing defeat for the Americans. Washington lost half of his men; his reputation, which rose and fell depending on whether he had just won or lost, was blackened.

The Canadian Campaign

Meanwhile, fighting on another front—an aspect of the war known as the Canadian Campaign—was heating up. Canada was a British possession that had been won from the French in 1763. In the late eighteenth century, most residents of Canada were Native Americans or people of French descent. During the American Revolution, the colonists tried to persuade Canada to become a "fourteenth colony" and join in America's rebellion against Great Britain.

But Canada was under the control of British soldiers and a popular governor, General Guy Carleton (1724–1808). Largely because of Carleton's influence, Canadians remained loyal to Great Britain. Hoping to make Canadians see things their way, the Continental Congress had authorized an invasion of Canada in June 1775.

The struggle was still going on a year later, when General John "Gentleman Johnny" Burgoyne (1722–1792) arrived in Montreal, Canada, from England, bringing British and German reinforcements to assist the embattled Carleton. Carleton was having a hard time of it; even though Canadians were loyal to Great Britain, they were passively loyal. They had shown no willingness to actively fight against the Americans. But with Burgoyne's reinforcements, the British were able to drive the Americans out of Canada.

Next, Burgoyne proposed a British invasion of America from Canada along the Lake Champlain-Hudson River route. After many delays, the plan was approved, and in June 1777, a confident Burgoyne launched what came to be known as "Burgoyne's Offensive." It would be an incredible journey—by boat, on foot, in wagons, and on horseback—through a wild and uncharted wilderness.

Burgoyne's Offensive, June-October 1777

Burgoyne commanded a force of about 10,500 British and German soldiers, Native Americans, and camp followers (see Chapter 7: Assembling an Army [1775–1776]). The offensive began well, with the easy capture of Fort Ticonderoga on Lake Champlain in early July 1777. (The fort had been taken from the British by Ethan Allen and Benedict Arnold two years earlier.) Burgoyne's contempt for American soldiers grew with the ease of his victory at Ticonderoga. American morale suffered badly at this defeat.

Burgoyne proceeded on his way to join forces with Howe at Albany, New York (in eastern New York State on the west bank of the Hudson River). The grueling trip from the Lake Champlain region to Fort Edward (in eastern New York on the northern tip of the Hudson) took about a month to complete. Mother Nature placed roadblocks in Burgoyne's way. He had to cut roads through pathless forests; he had to build bridges; and at one point he had to construct a two-mile-long log road across a swamp.

American patriots added obstructions of their own. Philip Schuyler (1733–1804) dispatched a thousand men with axes to cut down trees to block trails. They also dug ditches, making the already marshy pathways into virtual swamps, and pushed rocks into streams to make them overflow and to block the passage of boats. Burgoyne's exhausted party finally reached Fort Edward on July 29, 1777.

A little more than two weeks later, a large number of Burgoyne's German soldiers were killed or captured at nearby Bennington, Vermont. Burgoyne had sent them out to seize supplies and horses from the citizens of Vermont, because at this early stage of his offensive, he was already suffering shortages. Burgoyne had not anticipated this problem, and the events of the summer of 1777 pointed out three flaws in his great plan: First, he and his troops would have to resort to foraging and plundering the countryside for supplies because bringing supplies down from Canada was too difficult. Second, Burgoyne had hoped for support from the large numbers of Loyalists in New York, but they failed to turn out for him. According to Mark M. Boatner III "the Loyalists had an interesting effect on British strategic planners, who tended to count on finding stronger support ... [w]hen Tory support failed to materialize in New England the British expected to find it in New York. The hope of Loyalist assistance had a part in luring them into the unfortunate Bennington raid." Third, the local population was going to prove actively hostile and be a hindrance to his advance.

The more Americans saw of British and German soldiers, the more inclined they were to dislike them. News of the Jane McCrea tragedy (see Chapter 8: Native Americans and Blacks in the American Revolution) turned the population completely against the British. The defeat at Bennington was the beginning of the end for Burgoyne and his grand plan. From then on, the problem of feeding his army would grow even worse.

Burgoyne pressed on toward Albany, hoping to get relief from Howe. In early September of 1777, he crossed the Hudson River to Saratoga, New York. Later that month he was engaged by American generals Horatio (pronounced huh-RAY-shee-oh) Gates (c. 1728–1806) and Benedict Arnold (1741–1801; he had not yet turned traitor and joined the British) in the first of two famous battles of Saratoga at Freeman's Farm.

Battles at Saratoga, New York

By the time they reached Saratoga, Burgoyne's forces had dwindled to 5,700 men; there were many deaths and desertions due to hunger. Gates and Arnold surrounded Burgoyne with three times as many men. The fighting began on September 19, 1777, and it was fierce. Burgoyne waited for Howe to come to his aid, but he never did. Finally, when the situation seemed futile, Burgoyne called his generals together to discuss surrender. He asked them to consider three points: 1) Did military history offer any examples of a similar situation—an army surrendering when outnumbered, surrounded, low on food, and with retreat impossible? 2) Would a surrender under such circumstances be disgraceful? 3) Was Burgoyne's army now in a situation in which it had to surrender?

Burgoyne's generals answered "yes" to the first question; some obscure European battles were given as examples. The generals answered "no" to the second question. To the

John Burgoyne surrendered to General Horatio Gates on October 17, 1777. The American victory at Saratoga marked the turning point in the Revolution.
(Reproduced by permission of Archive Photos, Inc.)

third question, they replied that they were willing to fight to the death if they had any chance at all of winning; if nothing were to be gained by such a sacrifice, however, they felt that it would be better to surrender honorably and save some lives.

Burgoyne's surrender on October 17, 1777, was truly humiliating for him. America's victory at Saratoga marked the turning point in the Revolution. Twelve hundred British soldiers had died in the fighting there. After the dust of the Saratoga battles cleared, the British held only New York City, part of Rhode Island, and Philadelphia. They were unable to subdue either the American army or the people of the vast American countryside.

The sufferings at Saratoga

Frederika von Riedesel (pronounced REE-day-zel) was a German noblewoman—a baroness—who spent six years living in America during the time of the Revolutionary War. As the wife of the German general who accompanied British General John Burgoyne from Canada to Saratoga, she saw battles, was taken prisoner, nursed her children through illnesses, and maintained a brave and optimistic outlook. In *Letters and Journals Relating to the War of the American Revolution and the Capture of the German Troops at Saratoga*, a book comprised of the letters she wrote during that time, Riedesel offers a vivid picture of that eventful period in American history. In this passage, the baroness describes the aftermath of the first phase of the fighting at Saratoga, "a village of some thirty isolated houses."

> *On the 19th of September, there was an affair between the two armies.... I was an eye witness of the whole affair; and as I knew that my husband was in the midst of it, I was full of care and anguish, and shivered at every shot, for I could hear every thing. I saw a great number of wounded, and what was still more harrowing [distressing], they even brought three of them into the house where I was. One of these was Major Harnage.... He had received a shot through the lower part of the bowels, from which he suffered exceedingly. A few days after our arrival, I heard plaintive moans in another room near me, and I learned that they came from [an English officer by the name of] Young.... I went to him, and found him lying on a little straw.... He was a young man, probably eighteen or nineteen years old.... On account of his own sufferings he uttered no complaint. He had bled considerably, and they wished to take off his leg, but he could not bring his mind to it, and now [infection] had set in. I sent him pillows and coverings, and my women servants [sent him] a mattress. I redoubled my care of him, and I visited him every day, for which I received from the sufferer a thousand blessings. Finally, they attempted the amputation of the limb, but it was too late, and he died a few days afterward. As he occupied an apartment close to mine, and the walls were very thin, I could hear his last groans through the partition of my room.*

The baroness described how the inhabitants of the New York countryside fled at the approach of Burgoyne's party and rushed to join Gates's army. She pointed out that this ultimately led to Burgoyne's defeat at Saratoga, because every one of those who fled "was a soldier by nature, and could shoot very well; besides, the thought of fighting for their fatherland and their freedom ... inspired them with still greater courage."

The generals' critics

Even with news of the victory at Saratoga, the autumn of 1777 proved to be an especially difficult time for George Washington. He had always had his share of critics, but now many military experts of his era were voicing strong objections to the war strategies he had employed in the prior months. Historians have said that he should have marched north in July 1777, put down Burgoyne's invasion from Canada, returned with the additional northern troops, and stopped Howe before he took Philadelphia. Certain members of Congress were so disgusted with Washington that they secretly tried to get him removed from his command.

Some historians have speculated that a group of Washington's critics devised a plot, known as "Conway's Cabal" (pronounced kah-BALL), that aimed to have Washington replaced. (Other historians doubt that such a plot ever existed.) If successful, the cabal, or plot, would have allowed a group of New England congressmen to take over command of the American Revolution.

Around the time that American forces commanded by Gates were winning a great victory at Saratoga, Washington and his troops were stinging from their loss at Brandywine Creek. In this battle, the Americans were pushed back toward Philadelphia by British troops under Howe. This set the stage for the loss of the city of Philadelphia to the British. (See earlier section titled "Howe takes Philadelphia.") Among the influential Americans upset by Washington's retreat were Samuel Adams (1722–1803); Benjamin Rush (1745–1813), a respected army physician; Congressman Richard Henry Lee (1732–1794); and Thomas Mifflin (1744–1800), a general in the Continental army. These men and others criticized how Washington procured supplies, supervised his troops, and ran things on the battlefield. Washington's foes in Congress complained to all who would listen and sent around a paper that attacked both Washington's abilities and his popularity.

At this point, Thomas Conway (1735–c. 1800)entered the picture. Conway was an Irish-born officer in the French army who was fighting alongside the Americans in the Revolution. Having performed bravely at Brandywine, he boasted about himself and asked Congress to promote him to major general, although he was the most junior of the twenty-four generals serving in the American army. In a letter to Gates he wrote: "Heaven has been determined to save your country; or a *weak General* [referring to Washington] and bad Councellors would have ruined it."

Hearing about the letter, Washington was shocked that Conway and Gates were working together to discredit him. He wrote to Richard Henry Lee protesting the promotion of Conway. Washington claimed that such an appointment would have a disastrous effect on the morale of those soldiers who had served longer. He said he feared that some of his best officers might resign in disgust. According to John Rhodehamel in *George Washington, Writings,* Washington wrote in a letter to Lee: "I have been a Slave to the service: I have undergone more than most Men are aware of.... It will be impossible for me to be of any further service, if such ... difficulties are thrown in my way." When Washington learned that other patriots opposed him and his policies, he became angry and bitter towards them. He even threatened to resign from his job as head of the American army if the negative talk persisted.

Conway denied ever making the "weak general" statement; nonetheless, he offered his resignation to the Continental Congress. But foes of Washington in Congress pro-

Benjamin Franklin at the Court of France. In September 1776, Benjamin Franklin was one of three men appointed by Congress to go to Paris and ask the French for help in the Revolutionary War effort. This paved the way for France to enter the war. *(Reproduced by permission of Archive Photos, Inc.)*

Benjamin Franklin in Paris

Back in September 1776, Benjamin Franklin (1706–1790) was one of three men appointed by Congress to go to Paris and ask the French for help in the Revolutionary War effort. He was then seventy-years-old and had an international reputation as a scientist, inventor, writer, editor, and champion of the common man. The citizens of France may have loved Franklin, but King Louis XVI was not impressed. He did not think much of the Continental army and its record of losses, either. Louis wanted proof that America could defeat the British before he would commit himself to helping them. For more than a year, Franklin worked behind the scenes, discussing the American cause with the king's advisers and trying to arrange a meeting with the king himself. At last, on December 17, 1777, after hearing about the American victory at Saratoga and the fighting spirit shown by George Washington's soldiers, King Louis agreed to recognize American independence. This paved the way for France to enter the war.

The first French sailing fleet arrived in Virginia in July 1778. Franklin had accomplished his mission. When George Washington heard the news of the French alliance, he proclaimed "a day of rejoicing throughout the whole army." The American Revolution had become a world event.

moted Conway to the rank of major general. His job would involve a close working relationship with Washington. When Conway went to work alongside Washington, he was treated politely but very coldly. In a letter to Washington, Conway complained about not being received warmly and speculated that Washington would not support him in the carrying out of his duties. Washington forwarded the letter to Congress, admitting that he had a personal dislike for Conway but protesting that he never would have failed to support the man as claimed. Meanwhile, nine generals protested the promotion of Conway, declaring that he was not a talented military leader and that he was disliked and distrusted by other officers.

In the end, Conway and Gates claimed the original letter was harmless and offered to have it published. But they never offered to let Washington see it. Henry Laurens, president of the Continental Congress, wrote to a friend that he

had seen the letter. Though it did not contain the "weak general" phrase, what it did say about Washington was, according to Laurens, "ten times worse in every way." Finally, in an act that showed how Conway's Cabal had failed, Congress sent Gates back to the American army and Conway back to the French army. Washington was able to reestablish a good working relationship with Gates.

Howe had his critics, too. His decision to go to Philadelphia instead of helping Burgoyne at Saratoga stands as one of the major blunders in Great Britain's military history. Howe had not conquered Washington's army, nor had he destroyed Washington's will to fight on. In fact, American morale was growing. And in the eyes of the world, Washington and his troops were becoming worthy of admiration. They had shown they could overcome defeat and return to do battle again and again. In France, people began to refer to America's commander in chief as *le grand Washington* (the great Washington). When France's King Louis XVI (the sixteenth) heard

The winter at Valley Forge was the darkest time of the Revolution. George Washington (center) endured the harsh winter with his troops, while Howe spent a comfortable winter in Philadelphia.
(Reproduced by permission of The Library of Congress.)

During the bitter winter at Valley Forge, George Washington visited his sick and wounded soldiers. By the end of the harsh winter of 1778, a quarter of Washington's troops had died at Valley Forge.
(Reproduced by permission of Corbis Corporation [Bellevue].)

of Burgoyne's surrender at Saratoga, he finally agreed to join America in the war.

The winter at Valley Forge, December 19, 1777-June 1778

Howe spent a comfortable and lighthearted winter of 1777–1778 in Philadelphia. In eighteenth-century America's most sophisticated city, he attended plays, concerts, and balls, and he entertained the ladies, declaring them even more beautiful than the ladies of New York. Meanwhile, George Washington and his men suffered terribly at Valley Forge, Pennsylvania.

The winter at Valley Forge was the darkest time of the Revolution. During that brutal season, Washington wrote to Congress that 4,000 of his army of 11,000 men were "unfit for duty because they were bare foot and otherwise naked." James

Thacher (1754–1844), who was a surgeon for the Continental army, wrote a famous diary called the *Military Journal during the American Revolutionary War*. In it, he describes the problems facing Washington and his troops:

> *In the month of December the troops were employed in erecting log huts for winter quarters, when about one-half of the men were destitute of [shirts], shoes and stockings. Some thousands were without blankets, and were obliged to warm themselves over fires all night, after the fatigues [pronounced fa-TEEGS; tiring activities] of the day, instead of reposing in comfortable lodgings. At one time nearly three thousand men were [listed] unfit for duty from the want of clothing; and it was not uncommon to track the march of the men over ice and frozen ground by the blood from their naked feet. Several times ... they experienced little less than a famine in camp; and more than once our general officers were alarmed by the fear of a total dissolution [breaking apart] of the army from want of provisions.... Under these unexampled [never before seen or heard of] sufferings, the soldiers exercised a degree of patience and fortitude which reflects on them the highest honor, and which ought ever to entitle them to the gratitude of their country.... The commander-in-chief [General Washington] ... manifested a fatherly concern and fellow-feeling for their sufferings and made every exertion in his power to remedy the evil and to administer the much-desired relief. Being authorized by Congress, he reluctantly resorted to the unpopular [action] of taking provisions from the inhabitants by force, and thus procured a small supply for immediate necessity.*

By the end of the harsh winter of 1778, a quarter of Washington's troops had died at Valley Forge.

Sources

Books

Boatner, Mark M. III. *Encyclopedia of the American Revolution*. Mechanicsburg, PA: Stackpole Books, 1994.

Commager, Henry Steele, and Richard B. Morris, eds. *The Spirit of Seventy-Six: The Story of the American Revolution as Told by Participants*. New York: Da Capo Press, 1995.

Dolan, Edward F. *The American Revolution: How We Fought the War of Independence*. Brookfield, CT: Millbrook Press, 1995.

Flexner, James Thomas. *George Washington in the American Revolution (1775–1783)*. Boston: Little, Brown, 1968.

Hawke, David. *The Colonial Experience*. Indianapolis: Bobbs-Merrill, 1966.

Johnson, Paul. "The Role of Benjamin Franklin." In *A History of the American People*. New York: HarperCollins, pp. 134–42.

Jones, Robert F. *George Washington*. New York: Twayne, 1979.

Marrin, Albert. *The War for Independence: The Story of the American Revolution.* New York: Atheneum, 1988.

Rhodehamel, John, ed. *George Washington, Writings.* New York: Literary Classics of the United States, Inc., 1997.

Riedesel, Mrs. General. *Letters and Journals Relating to the War of the American Revolution and the Capture of the German Troops at Saratoga.* Translated from the original German by William L. Stone. Albany: Joel Munsell, 1867, pp. 114–15, 125.

Thacher, James. *Military Journal of the American Revolution* (one of several titles under which the book was published). Hartford, CT: Hurlbut, Williams & Co., 1862. Reprinted. New York: New York Times & Arno Press, 1969.

Trevelyan, George Otto. *The American Revolution.* Edited by Richard B. Morris. New York: David McKay Co., 1964.

Wheeler, Richard. *Voices of 1776.* New York: Thomas Y. Crowell, 1972.

Web Sites

"American Revolution Timeline: An Unlikely Victory, 1777–1783." The History Place. [Online] Available http://www.historyplace.com/unitedstates/revolution/revwar-77.htm (accessed on January 20, 2000).

The War Shifts to the South (1778–1780)

11

In the spring of 1778, William Howe (1729–1814) received word that his resignation as commander in chief of British forces in America had been accepted. He would be able to return to England as soon as his replacement, Henry Clinton (1738–1795), arrived in Philadelphia. The much-criticized Howe resigned because he felt that the British government had not sent him enough troops; without them, he said, he could not be expected to win the Revolutionary War.

In June 1778, Clinton learned that the French had joined forces with the Americans. Fearful that the French navy would cut him off from British headquarters in New York, Clinton quickly abandoned Philadelphia and headed for New York. George Washington (1732–1799) set up camp at West Point, New York.

For the next two years, there were no important battles in the North, although sporadic fighting did continue. New York and Pennsylvania were shocked by Indian raids. In the fall of 1778, Washington arranged his army in a semicircle around New York City, but Clinton did not respond to this maneuver. Clinton had decided to shift his fighting forces to

Henry Clinton arrived in Philadelphia in spring 1778, to relieve British General William Howe.
(Reproduced by permission of Archive Photos, Inc.)

the South, reasoning that England's best efforts in the North had failed.

The South in 1778

The Southern Colonies included Maryland, Virginia, North Carolina, South Carolina, and Georgia. The South was very different from the North socially, politically, and economically; its people even spoke differently. The vast and underpopulated terrain of the South ranged from swampy lowlands to forested wilderness, from pine barrens (expanses of white sand studded with pine trees) to large tracts of fertile farmland. Southern summers were unbearably hot, but the winters were mild and the growing season was long. The South boasted few towns and there was very little manufacturing. Instead, the economy revolved around farming.

More than a third of the Southern population consisted of black slaves. They worked on large tobacco plantations in Virginia and cultivated rice in Georgia and the Carolinas. Much smaller farms were cultivated by poor whites in Georgia and the Carolinas, while much of Maryland's large white Catholic population was employed in the mining and manufacturing of iron.

America was largely viewed by the outside world as a land of opportunity. In the North, at least, people could strive to rise in society; but in the South, there were rigid class divisions—the very rich, the very poor, and the black slaves. For the rich—who had earned their wealth by trading tobacco and cotton crops with England—the preservation of the *status quo* (present customs, practices, and power relations) was the main goal.

The British thought the South would be full of Loyalists—people who were loyal to King George III and to the way of life that had made them rich. If British soldiers and Southern Loyalists had combined their strength, they might have

Maßachußet, Jerßey — Riflemen. Artillerie

been able to defeat the Southern rebels in the American Revolution. But Great Britain's troops had been tied up in battle after battle in the North from 1775 to 1778. By the end of 1775, Southern rebels controlled the South, and that was the situation at the beginning of the Southern Campaign of 1778–80.

The Southern Campaign begins

The South had not seen any military action for two years, and the rebels had grown careless. In December 1778, Clinton sent British forces from New York to take Savannah, Georgia. It was easily captured and became the British center of Southern operations. In September-October of 1779, the patriots tried to take back Savannah with the help of the French navy. Their efforts failed, though, and patriot spirits sank. The British continued to hold Georgia.

Four uniforms worn by Revolutionary soldiers during the American Revolution. From left: First Rhode Island infantry man; a muskateer with a Napoleon-style hat; rifleman in buckskins; artilleryman holding wand (cannon tool) in his right hand. Drawing by Jean-Baptiste-Antoine de Verger. *(Reproduced by permission of Corbis Corporation [Bellevue].)*

By this time, the war had been going on for nearly five years. The American treasury was running dry, and soldiers were threatening to mutiny (rebel; leave the service) because they were not being paid, fed, or even clothed properly. British spirits were not much higher. They seemed to have gained very little after all their efforts. The French had declared war on England and French troops were attacking British possessions in the West Indies and other parts of the world. The British were desperate.

Charleston Expedition of 1779–80

Clinton had returned to New York in June 1779. Six months later, he and some 8,000 soldiers headed down to Charleston, South Carolina. It was a stormy thirty-eight-day voyage. Many of the British troops' horses, supplies, and artillery were lost as their ship, the *Anna*, "was blown across the Atlantic," noted Mark M. Boatner III in the *Encyclopedia of the American Revolution*.

Charleston was the major political and economic center of the South, home to 2,000 wealthy planters and their families—the richest group of people in America. Clinton's spirits brightened at the thought of a sure victory in Charleston. From there he sought to conquer the rest of the South.

Clinton finally moved against Charleston on February 11, 1780. The siege lasted three months. American General Benjamin Lincoln (1733–1810) and his 5,000 men were trapped and outnumbered by British sailors, redcoats, and Hessians (pronounced HESH-uns, German soldiers working for the British). Lincoln recounted his story, which was excerpted by Henry Steele Commager and Richard B. Morris in *The Spirit of Seventy-Six: The Story of the American Revolution as Told by Participants*. He vividly recalled the night of May 10, describing the enemy shells as "meteors crossing each other and bursting in the air; it appeared as if the stars were tumbling down." The general continued: "The fire was incessant almost the whole night; cannon-balls whizzing and shells hissing continually amongst us; ammunition chests ... blowing up; great guns bursting, and wounded men groaning along the lines. It was a dreadful night!" By May 12, they could hold out no longer,

Estimated Population of the American States: 1780

The first official census (count) of the population of the American states was conducted in 1790. Any figures prior to that date are estimates. This table shows estimates of the combined "white and Negro" population in 1780, then shows the estimated "Negro" population. Notice that an extremely large number of blacks lived in Virginia. Virginia was more unwilling than all the other colonies to arm blacks to serve in the American Revolution; slaveowners feared those guns would be turned against them in a massive slave uprising.

At the beginning of the Revolution, the population of Great Britain was 8 million, compared to an American population of about 2.75 million (20 percent of the people counted were slaves).

State* (1780)	White and Negro	Negro
Maine (counties)	49,133	458
New Hampshire	87,802	541
Vermont	47,620	50
Massachusetts	268,627	4,882
Rhode Island**	52,946	
Connecticut**	206,701	5,885
New York	210,541	21,054
New Jersey	139,627	10,460
Pennsylvania	327,305	7,855
Delaware	45,385	2,996
Maryland	245,474	80,515
Virginia	538,004	220,582
North Carolina	270,133	91,000
South Carolina	180,000	97,000
Georgia	56,071	20,831
Kentucky	45,000	7,200
Tennessee	10,000	1,500
Total	2,780,369	575,480

Notes: *The term "state" is used loosely here. There were thirteen "states"—former British colonies—when America declared its independence in 1776. Other settled areas farther west were referred to as "states," too, but there was no "union" of the States—or United States—until 1787. Delaware was the first state to ratify the U.S. Constitution; it was admitted to the Union on December 7, 1787. Vermont was admitted in 1791; Kentucky in 1792; Tennessee in 1796; and Maine in 1820.

**The "Negro" figures for Rhode Island and Connecticut include some Indians.

Source: Historical Statistics of the United States. *U.S. Bureau of the Census, Washington, D.C., 1960. In* Encyclopedia of the American Revolution, *by Mark M. Boatner III. Mechanicsburg, PA: Stackpole Books, 1994, p. 883.*

Charles Cornwallis (above) remained in Savannah, Georgia, while Clinton returned to New York. Constant quarreling between the two men further complicated the British campaign in the South. *(Reproduced by permission of Archive Photos, Inc.)*

and Lincoln surrendered. The loss of Charleston was the worst defeat in the entire war; it would remain America's biggest loss until the World War II Battle of Bataan (pronounced buh-TANN; occurred in the spring of 1942; a battle for a key island in the northern part of the Philippines that ended in Japanese victory and the capture of thousands of American and Filipino prisoners of war). The Carolinas now lay open to the British.

Cornwallis takes over Southern Campaign

Clinton returned to New York and stayed there, leaving Charles Cornwallis (1738–1805) in charge of Savannah. Clinton's Southern strategy up until this time (see box) caused many problems for Cornwallis. From this point until the fighting stopped in 1781, the British cause would be further complicated by constant quarreling between Clinton and Cornwallis. (Clinton was known for his poor relations with other commanding officers.) Cornwallis began a march through the Carolinas in his hoped-for conquest of the entire South.

Washington in 1780

Back up North, George Washington had spent the beginning of 1780—another awful winter—at his quarters in Morristown, New Jersey. Men deserted in droves, and Washington had to resort to repeated beatings and whippings to maintain discipline. The Hudson River froze. Private Joseph Plumb Martin wrote in his journal: "We were absolutely, literally starved.... I saw several of the men roast their old shoes and eat them, and I was afterwards informed by one of the officers' waiters, that some of the officers killed and ate a favourite little dog that belonged to one of them."

Henry Clinton's Southern Strategy

British General Henry Clinton believed he understood the Southern mind and had devised a strategy to win the South. His Southern strategy hinged on the longstanding hostilities that existed among Southerners. He hoped to "divide and conquer" the South by turning brother against brother and slave against owner.

Many Southern Loyalists were poor Scots and Irish farmers who were treated with contempt by both wealthy Loyalists and patriot Southerners. Once supplied with weapons by the British, however, poor Loyalists used them not to help in the war effort but to get revenge on their neighbors—Loyalists and patriots alike. In the horrible chaos that followed, innocent people were tortured, farms were burned to the ground, and homes were looted. None of this helped the British cause in the South.

Clinton contributed more fuel to the fire by issuing two famous proclamations. On June 30, 1779, he promised that "every Negro who shall desert the Rebel Standard [flag], [is granted] full security to follow within these Lines, any Occupation which he shall think proper." In response, tens of thousands of slaves fled behind British lines. This caused such a panic among Southern slaveowners that many decided to support the patriots.

The following year, on June 3, 1780, Clinton issued a proclamation releasing all prisoners from southern jails. Most would probably have gone home to sit out the war, but Clinton ordered them to take an oath of allegiance and actively support the British cause. This, in turn, prompted them to support the rebellion. Clinton's strategy had backfired.

Washington had not been home in six years. He had no money or supplies, and he began to wonder if the entire venture had been a mistake. Warmer weather brought a little relief. On July 10, 1780, 5,500 French troops under the command of Jean Baptiste Rochambeau (1725–1807) arrived at Newport, Rhode Island, and began to prepare for war. So far, the alliance with France had been a disappointment to the patriots, but this was about to change. Assisting Rochambeau in training French and American troops to fight together was Washington's young friend, the Marquis de Lafayette (1757–1834).

When Washington resumed his position, encircling the British in New York City, there was no response from Clinton. By

Supply Shortages Endanger Patriot Cause

Shortages of supplies, especially food, clothing, and shoes, began to be a problem for Washington's army as early as 1776. The situation grew worse and worse and continued until the last days of the war in 1781. Money shortages meant missed paydays, and serious morale problems resulted. Sometimes whole military units threatened to walk off the job, but their officers were usually able to talk them into returning to duty. When they could not persuade the men to return, sterner measures were sometimes employed. On one occasion, for example, Washington ordered three units of deserting New Jersey soldiers arrested. Three men in each unit were shot to serve as a warning to others who might be thinking about deserting.

Many people have wondered how—in a land of plenty—starvation and freezing could be such a problem for Washington's army. One answer is that supplies were available, but there was no way to get them to the troops: there were very few good roads; wagons were scarce; and if there were no rivers nearby, transporting goods was nearly impossible.

Another problem was that farmers and suppliers had lost their confidence in Continental money. They were afraid they would not be able to use it and, as a result, often refused to accept it. Some preferred to sell to the British in return for British money. It was not until 1781, with the war drawing to a close and a patriot victory seeming likely, that a renewed confidence in the nation's money supply helped the situation.

The Continental Congress has often been criticized for the way it oversaw the Revolutionary War (it was responsible for seeing to the payment of soldiers and the provision of supplies). According to military historian T. Harry Williams, though, "the accomplishment of the Congress was remarkable, and in the eighteenth century unexampled [without example; unprecedented]." He added: "Governments of that time did not engage in wars unless they had on hand a sufficient fund of coins to sustain their forces, a 'war chest' [money set aside to finance a war].... The Congress had no chest or any hope of acquiring one, but it still continued the war. It created its own money and decreed that all must use it in the national interest. And it kept its forces in the field and eventually won the war."

Source: T. Harry Williams. The History of American Wars from Colonial Times to 1918. New York: Alfred A. Knopf, 1981, pp. 21–39.

the end of 1780, the war in the North had reached a stalemate (standstill).

Fighting continues in the South

Although there was little action in the North, the South became a hotbed of activity. Beginning in December 1780, American General Nathanael Greene (1742–1786) engaged Cornwallis in a chase through the Southern swamps and into Virginia. Cornwallis tried to get the American army to stand up and fight, but the Americans eluded him. Greene displayed a sense of genius that would earn him a reputation second only to that of George Washington as a military commander. Cornwallis achieved some victories, but it could not be said that he won the South because he could not sway the people to his side. His soldiers plundered the countryside and behaved in such a reprehensible (shameful) manner that Southerners became outraged. Many were moved to join the fight against him.

Cornwallis's obstacles were overwhelming. The South was simply too large to be taken, he was constantly short of supplies, his Loyalist supporters lacked enthusiasm for fighting, and his commander, Clinton, failed to send him the reinforcements he needed so critically.

Changing strategies, Cornwallis decided that the seizure of Virginia would end the war, and in April 1781 he began to make his way there. Earlier, he had convinced General Clinton to send troops from New York to meet him in Virginia. At their head was the brilliant American General Benedict Arnold (1741–1801), who had recently stunned Washington and all of America by going over to the British side. The thought of Arnold and Cornwallis moving on Virginia focused George Washington's attention on the South.

George Washington as he looked in 1780. Painting by John Trumbull.
(Reproduced by permission of Corbis Corporation [Bellevue].)

Sources

Books

Boatner, Mark M. III. *Encyclopedia of the American Revolution.* Mechanicsburg, PA: Stackpole Books, 1994.

Commager, Henry Steele, and Richard B. Morris, eds. *The Spirit of Seventy-Six: The Story of the American Revolution as Told by Participants.* New York: Da Capo Press, 1995.

Dolan, Edward F. *The American Revolution: How We Fought the War of Independence.* Brookfield, CT: Millbrook Press, 1995.

Marrin, Albert. *The War for Independence: The Story of the American Revolution.* New York: Atheneum, 1988.

Martin, Joseph Plumb. *Yankee Doodle Boy: A Young Soldier's Adventures in the American Revolution Told by Himself.* Edited by George F. Scheer. New York: Holiday House, reissued 1995.

Williams, T. Harry. *The History of American Wars from Colonial Times to 1918.* New York: Alfred A. Knopf, 1981.

Web Sites

"American Revolution Timeline: An Unlikely Victory, 1777–1783." The History Place. [Online] Available http://www.historyplace.com/unitedstates/revolution/revwar-77.htm (accessed on January 20, 2000).

The Revolution Draws to a Close (1781–1783)

12

Former American General Benedict Arnold (1741–1801)—now fighting for the British—easily took Richmond, Virginia, on January 5, 1781. George Washington (1732–1799), commander in chief of American forces, responded by sending soldiers to Virginia under the command of the Marquis de Lafayette of France (1757–1834). (The French officially joined the war on the side of the Americans in 1778.) By the spring of 1781, British General Charles Cornwallis (1738–1805) had reached Richmond. Washington and his ally, French commander Jean Baptiste Rochambeau (1725–1807), decided to join Lafayette and trap Cornwallis in Virginia.

While he was still in New York, Washington devised a scheme to conceal his plan of heading to Virginia—he wanted to keep the British from sending more troops there. Washington arranged to leak false information to confuse General Henry Clinton (1738–1795), the commander in chief of British forces in America; it was a complete success. Thinking that the next battle would take place in New York, Clinton ordered Cornwallis to send every soldier he could spare to the Northeast. Over the next two months, Clinton changed his orders several times, confus-

Map of the Battle of Yorktown. *(XNR Productions. The Gale Group.)*

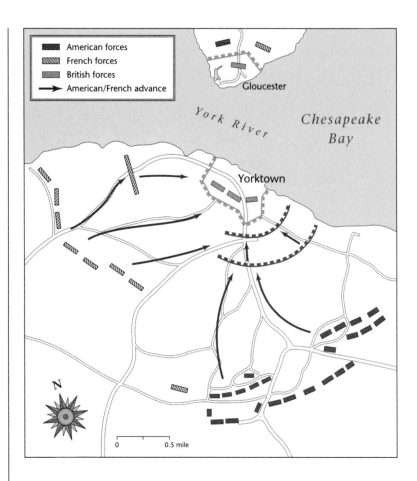

American forces
French forces
British forces
American/French advance

Gloucester

York River

Chesapeake Bay

Yorktown

N

0   0.5 mile

ing Cornwallis and his troops. Finally, in the intense heat of August 1781, a weary and disgusted Cornwallis settled in at Yorktown, Virginia, and began to fortify it against a possible attack. But by moving his 7,000 soldiers to Yorktown, the British general "put his back to the water [of the Chesapeake Bay] and made escape difficult—if not impossible," noted Edward F. Dolan in *The American Revolution: How We Fought the War of Independence.*

On August 21, 1781, Washington and Rochambeau began their march southward. Washington commanded about 8,800 men and Rochambeau had about 7,800. On September 5, a messenger brought word to Washington that a large and powerful French naval fleet had landed off the Virginia coast with reinforcements for Lafayette. Washington would have plenty of manpower in Yorktown.

French ships engaged British ships in a battle off the

coast of Virginia. The French inflicted severe damage on the British navy and insured there would be no help for Cornwallis from naval sources.

Surrender at Yorktown

On September 9, Washington reached his beloved home, Mount Vernon, in Virginia. He spent two nights there, then continued on to Yorktown. About two weeks later, the combined French and American armies surrounded Cornwallis's men (perhaps 7,000 to 8,000) at Yorktown. Cornwallis was unable to hold out against them. When General Clinton finally arrived at the mouth of the Chesapeake Bay with reinforcements for Cornwallis on October 24, he heard the news: General Cornwallis had surrendered the week before, on October 18, 1781.

Army surgeon James Thacher described the surrender scene in his journal entry dated October 19, 1781:

Washington and his ally, French commander Jean Baptiste Rochambeau (above), decided to join Marquis de Lafayette and trap British General Cornwallis in Virginia.
(Reproduced by permission of Corbis Corporation [Bellevue].)

> *This is to us a most glorious day, but to the English, one of bitter ... disappointment.... At about twelve o'clock, the combined army was arranged and drawn up in two lines extending more than a mile in length. The Americans were drawn up in a line on the right side of the road, and the French occupied the left. At the head of the former, the great American commander [George Washington], mounted on his noble courser [swift horse], took his station.... At the head of the latter was posted the excellent Count Rochambeau.... The French troops, in complete uniform, displayed a ... noble appearance.... The Americans, though not all in uniform, nor their dress so neat, yet exhibited an erect, soldierly air, and every countenance beamed with satisfaction and joy....*
>
> *It was about two o'clock when the captive [British] army advanced through the line formed for their reception. Every eye was prepared to gaze on Lord Cornwallis, the object of peculiar interest...; but he disappointed our anxious expectations; pretending [to be sick], he made General [Charles] O'Hara his substitute as the leader of his army.*

In this ceremony of surrender, the differences between the disciplined armies of the Old World and the undisciplined

Cornwallis surenders to the American troops at Yorktown on October 18, 1781. Painting by John Trumbull.
(Reproduced by permission of the National Archives and Records Administration.)

army of the New World were obvious. The soldiers of the British, German, and French armies looked magnificent in their colorful uniforms; some of the Frenchmen wore plumed hats and the chests of the officers glowed with stars and jewels. The Continental soldiers wore ragged hunting jackets of rough white cloth. The militiamen wore the clothing they had brought with them; many were barefoot.

As the defeated British and German soldiers moved between the two lines, their band played a slow, sad song. Legend says the song was "The World Turned Upside Down."

The news reaches London

News of the British defeat at Yorktown came as a complete surprise in London. King George III would not admit defeat and vowed to fight on. Yorktown was only one town, after all. The British still held New York and Charleston. What was to stop the king from sending more troops to America?

What stopped him were Parliament and British public opinion. Both had turned against the war. The House of Commons debated and passed the motion that "all further attempts to reduce the revolted colonies to obedience are contrary to [go against] the true interests of this Kingdom."

Treaty of peace is negotiated; Washington dismisses his army

British soldiers remained in New York for eighteen more months until the Treaty of Paris was worked out. In what is considered a triumph of skillful negotiating, Benjamin Franklin (1706–1790), John Jay (1745–1829), and John Adams (1735–1826) obtained for the new United States generous settlement terms—most importantly, independence, land, and the right to fish in international waters (the French had opposed granting America certain fishing rights). Benjamin Franklin tried but could not convince the British to give up Canada. The treaty was finally signed in Paris, France, on September 3, 1783.

Congress had ordered the Continental army to stay together until the treaty was signed. America's soldiers grew bored and restless and were enormously relieved to be disbanded in the fall of 1783. On November 3, Washington said farewell to his men. Although he had often been frustrated by their lack of discipline and respect, he had won a war with this hardy group of men. "The [disadvantages] ... under which the war was undertaken," Washington stated with pride, "can never be forgotten.... The unparalleled perseverance [determination] of the Armies of the United States, through almost every possible suffering and discouragement for the space of eight long years, was little short of a standing miracle." He further noted

THE COLONIAL GAZETTE

NUM. 39.]   SUPPLEMENT.   Price 2 Pence

Oct.   1781

LETTER FROM GEN. WASHINGTON TO THE GOVERNOR OF MARYLAND, ANNOUNCING THE SURRENDER OF CORNWALLIS.

CAMP NEAR YORK, OCT., 1781.

DEAR SIR : Inclosed I have the honor of transmitting to your Excellency the terms upon which Lord Cornwallis has surrendered the Garrisons of York and Gloucester.

We have not been able yet to get an account of prisoners, ordnance or stores in the different departments : but from the best general report there will be (officers included) upwards of seven thousand men, besides seamen, more than 70 pieces of brass ordnance and a hundred of iron, their stores and other valuable articles.

My present engagements will not allow me to add more than my congratulations on this happy event, and to express the high sense I have of the powerful aid which i have derived from the State of Maryland in complying with my every request to the execution of it. The prisoners will be divided between Winchester, in Virginia, and Fort Frederick, in Maryland. With every sentiment of the most perfect esteem and regard, I have the honor to be

Your Excellency's most obedient and humble servant,   G. WASHINGTON.

The French at Yorktown.

Few things, indeed, suggested by the history of the war are more instructive than a parallel between the fate of Burgoyne and the fate of Cornwallis. The defeat of Washington on Long Island and the loss of New York had been attributed to the fact that his troops were raw militia. Yet it was mainly with just such men, and not with Continentals (as the regular soldiers of the united colonies were called), that the American commanders in northern New York overcame, in two successive battles, the well-disciplined and admirably appointed army of Burgoyne. This was the one brilliant military triumph achieved by either party in the whole course of the struggle; yet, strange to say, its most substantial fruit was its favorable effect on the negotiations which for two years Franklin had been pushing at the court of Versailles. It was not, however, until the beginning of the ensuing year that the French Ministry would even promise assistance to the colonies; and although their advance of money may from that time forward be said to have kept the continental army on its feet, they did not render effective military aid until the arrival of Count De Grasse in the Chesapeake, about the beginning of September, 1781.

The surrender of Cornwallis was the direct result of the advantage gained by De Grasse over Admiral Graves in the naval battle which took place off the mouth of Chesapeake Bay on September 5, 1781. For the first time during the war, the English failed to have a preponderance of naval strength in American waters, and for almost the first time an English Admiral, commanding a force not greatly inferior to his opponents, sailed pusillanimously away after an indecisive action, in which the French loss is killed and wounded was actually the greater. After this unexpected and inexcusable behaviour on the part of an English naval officer, the surrender of Cornwallis was clearly an obvious necessity. On one side there was the French fleet, comprising twenty four ships of the line

carrying 1,700 guns, and 19,000 seamen. On the land side was Rochambeau with French troops, aggregating 8,400 men, and 3,600 Continental troops under Washington, together with 3,000 militia, who were of less account. Against this military and naval force, Cornwallis had 7,500 men within the works of Yorktown, exclusive of 800 marines, disembarked from some English frigate which had lain in the river. Under these circumstances the surrender of the English force was plainly a mere question of time. It may be said, however, that the presence of the land force at a place where it could so happily co operate with the French fleet, bears witness to great strategical ability, and it has been usual to give the credit of the combination to Washington. It is clear, however, that throughout the summer of 1781, the American commander had not seriously contemplated anything but a concerted attack on Sir Henry Clinton in New York. From the day, however, that De Grasse arrived in the Chesapeake, and notified the American and French commanders that he would take no ships no further northward, it required no great strategist to perceive that the land forces must operate in Virginia, if at all. It that moment the objective point of Washington and Rochambeau was palpably the force which Cornwallis, in obedience to Clinton, had collected at Yorktown. Cornwallis, on his part, became he counted on remaining on the peninsula, before, nor afterward, English fleet, and neither then, nor possible that an Admiral any Englishman have supposed it controlled would have edged himself bottled on the sea by Frenchmen till half of his army were sunk.

In view of these facts, it behooves us in this great celebration at Yorktown, to render our French visitors the honors they deserve, for the event commemorated is more truly and emphatically a French than an American achievement.

The front page of the October 1781 issue of "The Colonial Gazette" bears the headline "The French at Yorktown." This issue also included a letter from George Washington to the Maryland Governor, announcing the surrender of Cornwallis.

(Reproduced by permission of Corbis Corporation [Bellevue].)

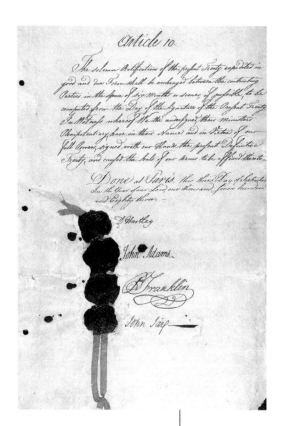

The Treaty of Paris, signed on September 3, 1783, ended the American Revolution. *(Reproduced by permission of Corbis Corporation [Bellevue].)*

that the events that led up to an American victory "have seldom if ever before taken place on the stage of human action, nor can they probably ever happen again," and concluded: "May the choicest of heaven's favours ... attend those who ... have secured unnumerable blessings for others; with these wishes, and this [blessing], the Commander in Chief is about to retire from Service. The ... military scene to him will be closed for ever."

How many served and died in the Revolutionary War?

There are varying estimates of the number of soldiers who served on the American side in the Revolutionary War. According to many historians, any such figures are unreliable, in part because leaders on both sides lied about the size of their forces to fool enemy spies. Author Paul Johnson estimated in *A History of the American People* that "at no point did [Washington's] total forces number more than 60,000." Many tried to get out of the service—either by sending substitutes or running away—but a large percentage of Revolutionary-era males performed at least some duty in the American military.

Military historian T. Harry Williams theorizes that a total of between 377,000 and 396,000 white Americans served at some point (but not all at once) in the Continental army, plus 5,000 black troops. He noted that these figures probably include militiamen who were counted more than once because they were called up to serve for short periods. Williams's figures also include men who signed up to get a bonus, deserted, and then signed up again. Perhaps 150,000 men served for a period of three years or longer.

The entire British army boasted 50,000 officers and troops at the outbreak of the war, but not all of them took part in the American Revolution. Great Britain had to keep part of her army at home for protection in case of attack by European nations. In addition, troops had to be stationed throughout Britain's far-flung empire, which included parts of India, the West Indies, and Canada. To add to her difficulties during the Revolutionary War, Britain's troops and supplies had to cross 3,000 miles of ocean, and the trip could take from two to four months.

King George III is said to have been dismayed (completely stunned) by news that his generals would need at least 50,000 troops to put down the rebellion in the colonies—that was the entire British force! The British government tried to meet this quota by the usual methods: taking volunteers and forcing the homeless to enlist. But the public was less than enthusiastic about serving in a faraway country. Ultimately, the king had to buy the services of 30,000 mercenaries (pronounced MER-suh-neh-reez; it means soldiers-for-hire), mostly from Germany (they were called Hessians; see Chapter 7: Assembling an Army [1775–1776]). He agreed to pay all the expenses of the German soldiers; he also agreed to pay a small sum for each soldier killed or wounded. This meant that after the first payment had been made, the soldiers were worth more dead than alive to their German princes.

By these means, then, Great Britain was able to sustain a force of about 35,000 men in America. Johnson calculates that they were aided by about 13,200 navy men and 13,000 Native Americans.

It is impossible to know for sure how many American soldiers died in the Revolution. According to military historian T. Harry Williams, the commonly accepted figures were 4,000 battle deaths and 10,000 deaths from all causes combined (such as smallpox). But historians were still debating the matter 200 years after the event. Williams noted that historian Howard H. Peckham estimated that 6,824 men were killed in battle, 10,000 died in camps, and 8,500 died as prisoners of war, for a total of 25,324 deaths. "If this estimate is correct," wrote Williams, "it makes the Revolution one of the deadliest wars in American history."

For More Information

Books

Boatner, Mark M. III. *Encyclopedia of the American Revolution*. Mechanicsburg, PA: Stackpole Books, 1994.

Catton, Bruce, and William B. Catton. *The Bold and Magnificent Dream: America's Founding Years, 1492–1815.* Garden City, NY: Doubleday, 1978.

Ferrie, Richard. *The World Turned Upside Down: George Washington and the Battle of Yorktown.* New York: Holiday House, 1999.

Kent, Zachary. *The Story of the Surrender at Yorktown.* Chicago: Childrens Press, 1989.

Middlekauff, Robert. *The Glorious Cause: The American Revolution, 1763–1789.* New York: Oxford University Press, 1982.

Web Sites

Hamill, John. "Revolutionary War Virtual Battlefield Tours." [Online] Available http://www.geocities.com/Pentagon/Bunker/8757/yorktown.html (accessed on February 14, 2000).

Sources
Books

Commager, Henry Steele, and Richard B. Morris, eds. *The Spirit of Seventy-Six: The Story of the American Revolution as Told by Participants.* New York: Da Capo Press, 1995.

Dolan, Edward F. *The American Revolution: How We Fought the War of Independence.* Brookfield, CT: Millbrook Press, 1995.

Flexner, James Thomas. *George Washington in the American Revolution (1775–1783).* Boston: Little, Brown, 1968.

Hawke, David. *The Colonial Experience.* Indianapolis: Bobbs-Merrill, 1966.

Johnson, Paul. *A History of the American People.* New York: HarperCollins, 1997.

Thacher, James. *Military Journal of the American Revolution* (one of several titles under which the book was published). Hartford, CT: Hurlbut, Williams & Co., 1862. Reprinted. New York: New York Times & Arno Press, 1969.

Williams, T. Harry. *The History of American Wars from Colonial Times to 1918.* New York: Alfred A. Knopf, 1981.

Web Sites

"American Revolution Timeline: An Unlikely Victory, 1777–1783." The History Place. [Online] Available http://www.historyplace.com/unitedstates/revolution/revwar-77.htm (accessed on January 20, 2000).

Where to Learn More

The following list focuses on general works about the Revolutionary era written for readers of middle school and high school age. Books aimed at adult audiences have been included when they are especially important in providing information or analysis that would otherwise be unavailable, or because they have become classics.

Blanco, Richard L., ed. *The American Revolution 1775–1783: An Encyclopedia.* New York: Garland Publishing, 1993.

Cox, Clinton. *Come All You Brave Soldiers: Blacks in the Revolutionary War.* New York: Scholastic, 1999.

Egger-Bovet, Howard, and Marlene Smith-Baranzini. *USKids History: Book of the American Revolution.* Boston: Little Brown & Co., 1994.

Faragher, John Mack, ed. *The Encyclopedia of Colonial and Revolutionary America.* New York: Facts on File, 1990.

Fleming, Thomas. *Liberty! The American Revolution.* New York: Viking Penguin, 1997. (Companion volume to the PBS television series.)

Hakim, Joy. *From Colonies to Country.* Vol. 3, *A History of the U.S.* New York: Oxford University Press, 1993.

Hibbert, Christopher. *Redcoats and Rebels: The American Revolution Through British Eyes.* Dresden, TN: Avon Books, 1991.

King, David C. *Lexington and Concord.* New York: Twenty-First Century Books, 1997.

Leckie, Robert. *George Washington's War: The Saga of the American Revolution.* New York: HarperCollins, 1992.

Lukes, Bonnie L. *The American Revolution.* World History Series. San Diego, CA: Lucent Books, 1996.

Meltzer, Milton. *The American Revolutionaries: A History in Their Own Words 1775–1800.* New York: Crowell, 1987.

Nardo, Don, ed. *The American Revolution.* Opposing Viewpoints Digests. San Diego, CA: Greenhaven Press, 1998.

O'Neill, Laurie. *The Boston Tea Party.* Spotlight on American History. Brookfield, CT: Millbrook Press, 1996.

Purcell, L. Edward. *Who Was Who in the American Revolution.* New York: Facts on File, 1993.

Reit, Seymour. *Guns for General Washington: A Story of the American Revolution.* Great Episodes. San Diego, CA: Harcourt Brace, 1992.

Stein, R. Conrad. *Cornerstones of Freedom: The Story of Valley Forge.* Chicago: Children's Press, 1985.

Stokesbury, James L. *A Short History of the American Revolution.* New York: William Morrow & Co., 1992.

Whitney, David C., and Robin Vaughan Whitney. *The American Presidents.* 8th ed. Pleasantville, NY: Reader's Digest Association, 1993.

Wilbur, C. Keith. *The Revolutionary Soldier, 1775–1783: An Illustrated Source Book of Authentic Details About Everyday Life for Revolutionary War Soldiers.* Philadelphia: Chelsea House, 1996.

Index

Illustrations are marked by (ill.)

C

D

E

F

G